III

Obsessive-Compulsive Disorder Across the Life Cycle

III

Obsessive-Compulsive Disorder Across the Life Cycle

Contents

Section III

Obsessive-Compulsive Disorder Across the Life Cycle

Foreword

Michele T. Pato, M.D., and Gail Steketee, Ph.D.,
Section Editors

It is particularly relevant to study obsessive-compulsive disorder (OCD) throughout the life cycle, because for many suffering with OCD, it is a chronic illness beginning in childhood and continuing into later life.

In reading Chapters 11 through 13 of this section—OCD in Children and Adolescents (Drs. Penn, March, and Leonard), in Adults (Drs. Pato and Pato), and in Later Life (Drs. Pollard, Carmin, and Ownby)—the reader should be struck most by the persistence and similarity of symptoms, as well as the comparable prevalences of the disorder, across the life cycle. In addition, the same treatments are effective in different age groups. With regard to pharmacological treatment in particular, it is notable that although dosage adjustments are needed depending on age, a relatively long treatment duration—beginning with 10–12 weeks in the initial treatment phase—seems to be indicated at all stages of the life cycle.

It is generally believed that any stress can cause an exacerbation of OCD symptoms. Thus, it is not surprising to find, in Chapter 15 (by Diaz, Grush, Sichel, and Cohen), that pregnancy and the puerperium—life-cycle events of particular importance for many women—can be a time of worsening obsessive-compulsive symptoms. This finding runs counter to the traditional belief that pregnancy is a period of relative mental well-being.

Chapter 14 (Drs. Eisen and Steketee) reinforces and extends the notion established by the other chapters in this section—namely, that OCD is a lifelong illness and that relatively few patients experience a total disappearance of symptoms over time. More than anything, this chapter highlights the work that still needs to be done to identify factors that contribute to and predict OCD course and outcome.

Chapter 11

Obsessive-Compulsive Disorder in Children and Adolescents

Joseph V. Penn, M.D., John March, M.D., M.P.H., and Henrietta L. Leonard, M.D.

Only 10 years ago, the perception existed that obsessive-compulsive disorder (OCD) was rare in childhood. Psychiatrists saw few patients, perhaps because of the secretive nature of the disorder or the reluctance of patients, or because OCD symptoms were not appropriately recognized or treated. It is now estimated that perhaps as many as 1 million children and adolescents in this country may suffer from OCD. Similar to adults, children with OCD often have their symptoms for quite a while before they receive assessment and treatment. Families may turn first to nonpsychiatric specialists, who have varying degrees of experience with the disorder, which may further delay recognition and treatment. With increasing professional and media interest in this disorder and greater sensitivity to its diagnosis, many people with OCD are now receiving accurate diagnoses and effective treatments. In this chapter we review the phenomenology, diagnosis, etiology, and treatment issues of OCD in children and adolescents. Pediatric pharmacological treatment and cognitive-behavior therapy of OCD is emphasized. Also presented is recent evidence for a subtype of pediatric-onset OCD.

Phenomenology

Symptoms

In DSM-IV (American Psychiatric Association 1994), as in DSM-III-R (American Psychiatric Association 1987), OCD is characterized by recurrent obsessions and/or compulsions that are severe enough to "cause marked distress or significant impairment" (American Psychiatric Association 1994, p. 417). An affected child or adolescent must have either obsessions or compulsions, although the majority seem to have both. DSM-IV specifies that affected individuals must recognize at some point in the illness that their obsessions are not simply excessive worries about real problems; and, similarly, compulsions must be seen as excessive or unreasonable, although this condition may not always hold true for young children. A change in the DSM-IV criteria from those in DSM-III-R specifies that persons of all ages who lack insight receive the added specification *poor insight type*. The specific content of the obsessions cannot be related to another Axis I diagnosis, such as preoccupations about food resulting from an eating disorder or guilty thoughts (ruminations) from major depressive disorder.

Children and adolescents with OCD typically have both obsessions and compulsions (Flament et al. 1988; Judd 1965; Riddle et al. 1990b; Swedo et al. 1989b). An individual typically attempts to ignore, suppress, or neutralize the intrusive obsessive thoughts. Generally, compulsions are carried out to dispel anxiety and/or in response to an obsession (e.g., to ward off harm to someone). Berkowitz and Rothman (1960) described obsessions in children that varied greatly, ranging from an ideational wish that misfortune or death would befall a parent to bizarre, unrealistic, persistent thoughts. The most commonly reported obsessions focus on concerns about germs and contamination, fears about harm or danger, worries about right and wrong, or having a "tune in the head" (Swedo et al. 1989b). The major presenting ritual symptoms include (in order of decreasing frequency) excessive "cleaning" (hand washing, showering, bathing, or tooth brushing); repeating rituals (going in and out doors, getting up from and sitting down on chairs, restating phrases, or rereading); checking behaviors (making sure that doors and windows are locked, that appliances are turned off, or that homework is done "right"); counting; ordering/arranging; touching; and hoarding (Flament et al. 1988; Judd 1965; Rettew et al. 1992; Riddle et al. 1990b; Swedo et al. 1989b). Some of the obsessions and rituals involve an internal sense that "it doesn't feel right" until the thought or action is completed.

In contrast to other forms of psychopathology, the specific symptoms of OCD are essentially identical in children and adults (Hanna 1995; Rapoport 1986; Rettew et al. 1992; Swedo et al. 1989b). The individual types of obsessions and compulsions have been reported to be numerous although of a finite type and to change in both content and severity over time in most individuals (Rapoport 1989; Swedo et al. 1989b). Rettew and colleagues (1992) studied the individual OCD symptoms of 79 children and adolescents with severe OCD over an average of 7.9 years (range 2–16 years) and found no significant relationships with either the number or the type of OCD symptoms and age. Despite a diversity in symptoms, the symptom "pool" was remarkably finite and very similar to that seen in adults. Most OCD patients simultaneously experience several OCD symptoms, which change over time. This finding would argue against a unique, specific symptom content (e.g., obsessions versus rituals, washing versus checking) being representative of a subgroup (phenotype) of OCD.

Age and Gender Effects

Seventy consecutive child and adolescent patients were prospectively examined at the National Institute of Mental Health (NIMH) (Swedo et al. 1989b). These 47 boys and 23 girls met diagnostic criteria for primary severe OCD, and had a mean age at onset of illness of 10 years of age. Seven of the patients had the onset of their illness prior to age 7. Boys tended to have an earlier (prepubertal) onset, usually around age 9, whereas girls were more likely to have a later (pubertal) illness onset, around age 11. Interestingly, the children with an earlier onset of OCD were more likely to be male and to have a family member with OCD or a tic disorder. Patients with a very early onset of OCD (less than 6 years old) were more likely to have compulsions than obsessions, and their symptoms (such as blinking and breathing rituals) tended to be more unusual than the classic OCD symptoms.

There is some disagreement regarding the gender distribution of children and adolescents with OCD. Although a preponderance of males is seen in most studies of children and adolescents with OCD, two epidemiological studies of OCD in adolescents and two studies of referred children and adolescents with OCD found an approximately equal number of males and females with OCD (for a review, see Hanna 1995). This finding is most likely explained by the fact that in the prepubertal years, there is a higher male-to-female ratio for the disorder, whereas postpubertally this ratio is reversed. At least one-third of adults with OCD have reported to have first developed the disorder in childhood (Black 1974), often at a very early age. Age at onset can range from 3 to 18 years (Riddle et al. 1990b) but is typically 9 to 11 years (Last and Strauss 1989), or 7 to 18 years with a mean age at onset of 12.8 years (Flament et al. 1988). Several studies suggest that boys have an earlier age at onset than girls (Flament et al. 1985; Last and Strauss 1989; Swedo et al. 1989b), that younger boys have more severe symptoms than younger girls (Flament et al. 1988), and that boys are more likely than girls to have a comorbid tic disorder (Leonard et al. 1992). It has been suggested that earlier onset of illness may be associated with increased genetic loading (Lenane et al. 1990; Leonard et al. 1992; Pauls et al. 1995).

OCD is characterized by a waxing and waning course, often with worsening related to psychosocial stressors. Children will often initially disguise their rituals (Swedo et al. 1989b). Severely incapacitated children and adolescents with hallmark OCD symptoms will be more readily diagnosed. Less severely ill patients, and those attempting to hide symptoms, are more difficult to recognize. "Red flags" for OCD may include lengthy, unproductive hours spent on homework, holes erased into test papers and homework, or retracing over letters or words. Unexplained high utility bills, a dramatic increase in laundry, an insistence on wearing clothes or using a towel only once, or toilets being stopped up from too much paper may alert the family to an obsession about germs and contamination. Behaviors suspicious for OCD include lengthy bedtime rituals; exaggerated requests for reassurance; difficulty leaving the house; peculiar patterns for walking, breathing, or sitting; requests for family members to repeat phrases; a recurring fear of harm coming to oneself or others; or a persistent fear that one has an illness. Finally, hoarding seemingly useless objects such as magazine subscription coupons, empty juice cans, or street garbage requires differentiation from normal childhood behavior of collecting rocks, sticks, or other sentimental "treasures."

Few rating scales are available to assess OCD severity in children or adolescents. The Children's Yale-Brown Obsessive Compulsive Scale (CY-BOCS; Goodman et al. 1992) has been specifically adapted for children and is the most widely used. The CY-BOCS can document baseline severity of symptoms and changes over time that otherwise might not be reported unless specifically assessed. Part of this scale, the Y-BOCS Symptom Checklist, is particularly useful in a clinical interview to elicit all the symptoms, including more "minor" and more secretive ones that might go unnoticed or undisclosed.

Epidemiology

Initial estimates of the incidence of childhood OCD were derived from psychiatric clinic populations. Berman (1942) reported "obsessive-compulsive phenomena" in 6 of 2,800 (0.2%) patients. Hollingsworth and colleagues (1980) found 17 cases of OCD in 8,367 (0.2%) child and adolescent inpatient and outpatient records. Judd (1965) conducted a retrospective chart review study that revealed 5 cases in 425 (1.2%) pediatric records.

The first epidemiological study, the Isle of Wight study, reported "mixed obsessional/anxiety disorders" in 7 of 2,199 (0.3%) 10- and 11-year-old children surveyed (Rutter et al. 1970). Flament and colleagues (1988) found a (weighted point) prevalence rate of 0.8% and a lifetime prevalence of 1.9% in a whole-population adolescent epidemiology study. These data suggest that OCD is a relatively common disorder in adolescence. Furthermore, this is compatible with both the estimated prevalence in the general population (Karno et al. 1988) and the finding that at least one-third to one-half of adult OCD patients first developed the illness in childhood (Black 1974).

Differential Diagnosis

The differential diagnosis of OCD is broad and includes the depressive and anxiety disorders (separation anxiety, simple phobia, social phobia, panic disorder, and generalized anxiety disorder) with obsessional features; stereotypies seen in mental retardation, pervasive developmental disorders (PDDs), autism, and brain damage syndromes; obsessive-compulsive personality disorder (OCPD); anorexia and bulimia; tic disorders; and, more rarely, childhood schizophrenia. Obsessive brooding and ruminating may be demonstrated in major depressive disorder, but the thoughts are usually more content specific and are not seen as senseless. Fear of harm coming to oneself or others can be found in separation anxiety disorder, but in OCD this specific thought usually results in the need to perform compulsive rituals. Similarly, the excessive and unrealistic worry in generalized anxiety disorder is not accompanied by classic compulsive rituals. Avoidance secondary to simple phobia does not usually involve germs as a primary object of avoidance; and the phobic person's fear usually decreases when he or she is not confronted with the stimuli, unlike the case in OCD. The relationship between OCPD and OCD remains unclear for children as well as for adults, and merits more study.

Although repetitive, formalized behaviors such as the stereotypies seen in children and adolescents with autism, mental retardation, PDD, or organic brain damage may superficially resemble OCD rituals, OCD rituals are typically well organized, complex, and ego-dystonic. In autism, the rituals seem reassuring, lack ego-dystonicity, and are not associated with an obsession. Other features of autism, such as peculiar speech patterns and severely impaired interpersonal relationships, are not seen in OCD (Swedo and Rapoport 1989). Rigid and repetitive behaviors of Asperger's syndrome may appear to resemble those seen in OCD. A careful assessment of developmental history, clinical presentation, social relationships, and symptoms may be helpful in making the distinction between stereotypies and OCD rituals.

The anorexic or bulimic patient's consuming or "obsessive" interest in calories, exercise, and food and "compulsive" avoidance, measuring, and monitoring of food may certainly bear a resemblance to symptoms of OCD. Although OCD and eating disorders may coexist, the distinction can usually be made between OCD and a primary eating disorder, because when considered in context, the focus of the obsessions and compulsions in eating disorders are all related to food and body image.

Associated Disorders

Disorders most commonly associated with childhood OCD follow patterns somewhat similar to those reported in adults, with affective and anxiety disorders most common (Swedo et al. 1989b). However, attention-deficit/hyperactivity disorder (ADHD) and behavioral disorders may be more prevalent in children. In the 70 consecutive children studied at the NIMH, comorbidity was common, with only 18 (26%) having no other psychiatric diagnosis (Swedo et al. 1989b). At initial presentation, the children and adolescents had the following concurrent diagnoses: tic disorder (30%), major depression (26%), specific developmental disability (24%), simple phobia (17%), overanxious disorder (16%), adjustment disorder with depressed mood (13%), oppositional disorder (11%), attention-deficit disorder (10%), conduct disorder (7%), separation anxiety disorder (7%), enuresis (4%), alcohol abuse (4%), and encopresis (3%) (Swedo et al. 1989b).

Hanna (1995) found that lifetime rates of depressive, anxiety, disruptive behavior, and tic disorders ranged from 26% to 32%. Depression is frequently associated with OCD, with secondary depression developing in response to distress and interference from OCD. Phobias and anxiety disorders may also occur concurrently with OCD. Riddle and colleagues (1990b) found that among children without preexisting major neuropsychiatric disorders, the rates of comorbid anxiety and mood disorder diagnoses were relatively high.

Patients with Tourette's syndrome (TS) often have associated obsessive-compulsive symptomatology and/or meet full DSM-IV OCD criteria (Cohen and Leckman 1994; Frankel et al. 1986; Leckman et al. 1993; Leonard et al. 1992; Pauls et al. 1986). It is important to carefully distinguish between rituals and tics, as each requires different treatments. In general, OCD patients' rituals are more complex and occur in response to an obsession. Thus, if an action is preceded by a specific cognition and is performed to "undo" or "dispel" the thought, it is considered to be a compulsive ritual. Some complex motor tics may be preceded by tension, a sensation, or an "urge"; however, they are not typically initiated by a thought or accompanied by anxiety. On rare occasions, a complex motor tic preceded by a cognition, sensation, or urge may be difficult to distinguish from a compulsive ritual (Leckman et al. 1994). These experiences may include premonitory feelings or urges that are relieved with the performance of the act and a need to perform tics or compulsions until they are felt to be "just right." For a more detailed discussion, readers are referred to Leckman et al. (1993, 1994).

ADHD may also occur concurrently with OCD, and appears to have a higher frequency in male patients (Hanna 1995; Riddle et al. 1990b; Swedo et al. 1989b). Hanna (1995) found that one-third of 31 children and adolescents with OCD also had a current disruptive behavior disorder (DBD). The ADHD arose before the OCD, whereas the oppositional defiant and conduct disorders tended to develop in conjunction with the OCD. Geller and colleagues (1995) found that DBDs were among the most common comorbid diagnoses in their sample of 38 patients with OCD. In addition to the greater severity of OCD illness in patients with a prepubertal onset, increased rates of comorbid DBD are seen, although DBDs are generally more common in boys than in girls (Anderson et al. 1987).

Etiology

The etiology of OCD is unknown, but research suggests frontal lobe–limbic–basal ganglia dysfunction (Insel 1992; Wise and Rapoport 1989). Additionally, neurotransmitter dysregulation, genetic susceptibility, and environmental triggers appear to have roles in the pathogenesis of the illness. The demonstration that serotonin reuptake inhibitors (SRIs) are specifically efficacious in the treatment of OCD has led to the "serotonin hypothesis" of OCD. However, it is unlikely that neurotransmitter dysregulation can be attributed to only one system, given that others (e.g., dopamine) have also been implicated. For an excellent review, the reader is referred to Insel (1992).

Additional evidence supports a neurobiological etiology of OCD, which includes neuroanatomical, neurophysiological, and neuroimmunological associations and metabolic abnormalities. Head injury, brain tumors, carbon monoxide poisoning, and other brain insults resulting in basal ganglia damage have been reported to be related to the onset of OCD symptomatology (Insel 1992). Basal ganglia diseases, such as postencephalitic Parkinson's disease (von Economo 1931) and Huntington's chorea (Cummings and Cunningham 1992), also have an increased rate of OCD. Neuroimaging studies in adult OCD patients with a childhood onset of symptoms compared with nonimpaired control subjects have shown decreased caudate size on computed tomography (CT) scans (Luxenberg et al. 1988) and abnormal patterns of regional glucose metabolism on positron-emission tomography (PET) scans (Swedo et al. 1989c, 1992).

Generally, pediatric OCD probands do not appear to have either gross or clinically impairing neurological or neuropsychological abnormalities, although "soft signs" may be present. Minor perinatal or premorbid developmental problems were reported for several children and adolescents in Riddle and colleagues' phenomenology study (1990b); however, none of the children had a major perinatal or developmental problem that appeared to have an obvious relationship to the onset or course of OCD. In general, the children with OCD performed comparably with the control subjects on neuropsychological measures; however, increased errors produced on a select subset of tests were interpreted to be consistent with frontal lobe or caudate lesions or both (Cox et al. 1989). On stressed neurological examination of 54 pediatric OCD patients, more than 80% had some positive "soft" neurological finding (Denckla 1989). The subtle findings on stressed neurological examination and on complete neuropsychological testing are suggestive of underlying abnormalities. Children with OCD who show specific abnormalities in visual-spatial-organizational information processing are at risk for specific learning problems, such as dysgraphia, arithmetic and expressive written-language deficiencies, and slow processing speed and efficiency (J. March and C. K. Conners, unpublished data). When poor social skills resulting from weaknesses in the nonverbal processing of social-emotional communication are also present (J. March, unpublished data), OCD may overlap Asperger's syndrome. These subtle neuropsychological and academic impairments may be missed and may contribute clinically to "treatment-resistant" cases.

Intriguing links have also been found among TS, tic disorders, and OCD. Patients with TS frequently have obsessive-compulsive features, and OCD patients have an increased incidence of tic disorders (Leonard et al. 1992; Pauls et al. 1986). Since the initial systematic family study of probands with TS (Pauls et al. 1986), other studies have demonstrated increased rates of OCD in families of probands with TS and increased rates of tic disorders in families of probands with OCD (Leonard et al. 1992). A number of studies have demonstrated familial links among OCD, tic disorders, and TS (see Pauls et al. 1986, 1995), suggesting a genetic vulnerability for OCD and tic disorders. Pauls and colleagues (1986) hypothesized that OCD and TS may be different manifestations of the same gene(s). Walkup and colleagues (1995) recently proposed a mixed model of inheritance. OCD probands often have a family history of tic disorders and OCD, and TS probands often have a family history of tic disorders and OCD. Lenane and colleagues (1990) found that 20% of personally interviewed first-degree relatives of children and adolescents with OCD also met lifetime history criteria for OCD. Of note, the primary OCD symptom in the affected family member was usually different from that in the proband, a finding arguing against both a modeling theory for OCD and familial symptom subtypes.

Holzer and colleagues (1994) compared the phenomenological features of 35 adult OCD patients with a lifetime history of tics and those of age- and sex-matched OCD patients without tics. They found that the OCD patients with tics had more touching, tapping, rubbing, blinking, and staring—and fewer cleaning—rituals but did not differ from the non-tic OCD patients on obsessions. Continued studies of OCD symptom phenomenology may reveal that those with a lifetime history of a chronic tic disorder represent a potential subtype (Goodman et al. 1990). Similarly, McDougle and colleagues (1994) also described a possible subtype of OCD. They studied the efficacy of adding haloperidol to the treatment regimens of OCD patients with or without a comorbid chronic tic disorder who were refractory to adequate treatment with the selective serotonin reuptake inhibitor (SSRI) fluvoxamine. Their study suggested that OCD patients with a comorbid tic disorder constitute a subtype of OCD that might require conjoint SSRI and dopamine-blocking-agent therapy for effective symptom reduction.

Pauls and colleagues' (1995) family study described OCD as being a heterogeneous disorder with some cases being genetically mediated. They found that rates of OCD and subthreshold OCD were significantly greater among the relatives of the probands with OCD than among comparison subjects. They also found that children with onset of OCD between 5 and 9 years of age had a much higher rate of family members with tics, suggesting an increased genetic loading. Their study supported a previous hypothesis that earlier-onset cases of OCD represent more severe forms of disease (at least in terms of risk to relatives) (Leonard et al. 1992).

Heterogeneity of pediatric OCD has been described, and a large phenomenological study showed that some children have an abrupt onset, some have a dramatic and episodic course, and some exhibit coexisting choreiform movements. In recent years, parallel studies of Sydenham's chorea (SC) (Allen et al. 1995; Swedo et al. 1989a, 1993, 1994) and OCD have been conducted; these have demonstrated that a subgroup of OCD children first developed their OCD symptoms after a Group A beta-hemolytic streptococcal infection (GABHS) (Swedo 1994). There have been exciting research developments regarding the relationship between OCD and SC. SC is the neurological variant of rheumatic fever and is characterized by an autoimmune response in the region of the basal ganglia caused by misdirected antibodies from a streptococcal infection (Swedo et al. 1989a, 1993). There is an increased incidence of OCD in pediatric patients with SC, and it has been hypothesized that SC serves as a medical model for OCD (Swedo et al. 1989a). Recently, a subgroup of children with a pediatric onset of either OCD or a tic disorder has been described (pediatric autoimmune neuropsychiatric disorders associated with streptococcal infection [PANDAS]). These patients are characterized by an abrupt prepubertal onset of their symptoms after a GABHS and by a course of illness characterized by alternating periods of remission and dramatic, acute worsening of symptoms. This group likely represents a genetic vulnerability different from that associated with later-onset OCD. PANDAS children often have neurological signs such as choreiform movements and tics. These children appear to have an underlying pathophysiology similar to that seen in SC, although they do not have SC.

It is critical to delineate this prepubertal pediatric subtype, as these patients require a different assessment and treatment. A child presenting with an acute onset of OCD with or without tics, or a significant deterioration, requires a thorough assessment and evaluation of recent or concomitant medical illnesses, including seemingly benign upper-respiratory-tract infections. Laboratory analyses such as a throat culture, an antistreptolysin O (ASO) titer, and an antinuclear antibody test (which may be nonspecifically positive) may be helpful in diagnosing GABHS infections.

Thus, evidence suggests that early (prepubertal)-onset OCD may represent a meaningful OCD subtype. Interestingly, Ackerman and colleagues (1994) found age at OCD onset to be a strong predictor of response to clomipramine in adults. People who develop OCD later in life appear to have a better chance of responding than do those who become ill earlier, independent of length of illness, again providing indirect evidence that early onset may represent a more severe and less responsive form of the illness. The association between age at the time of onset and response to clomipramine may indicate a basic difference in the pathology of the disorder.

The successful integration of these neuroanatomical and neurophysiological hypotheses of childhood OCD with theories of genetic susceptibility and environmental stressors will generate additional research questions.

Treatment

Selection of Treatment(s)

Children and adolescents with OCD vary significantly with respect to the specific nature of the OCD and its impact. Thus, each child or adolescent requires a comprehensive individualized assessment of symptoms, comorbidity, and psychosocial factors. For an excellent reference on the general clinical assessment of the child, the reader is referred to King (1995). The individualized treatment plan should take into consideration the unique psychosocial and family issues that may influence compliance and treatment response. Whenever possible, both the patient and his or her family should participate in the development of treatment plans.

Psychodynamic Psychotherapy

Whether particular OCD symptoms represent specific intrapsychic conflicts is debatable. Esman (1990) eloquently described how OCD can be understood as having both biological and psychodynamic components. Jenike (1990) reviewed psychotherapeutic interventions available for OCD and concluded that "the traditional psychodynamic psychotherapy is not an effective treatment for patients with OCD as defined in DSM-III-R, as there are no reports in the psychiatric literature of patients who stopped ritualizing when treated with this method alone" (p. 113). Psychodynamic psychotherapy may play an important role by addressing specific issues in a patient's life—for example, the impact of the illness on the patient's self-esteem, relationships, and other psychosocial conflicts—and by improving compliance with the behavioral or pharmacological treatments that deal more directly with OCD symptomatology.

Individual and Family Therapy

Psychotherapy may play an important role in teaching coping skills, addressing comorbid diagnoses and family issues, treating the accompanying anxiety and depressive symptoms of OCD, and helping to improve peer and family relationships. Because families affect and are affected by OCD, family members often need assistance and direction in how to effectively participate in pharmacological and behavioral treatment. Thus, a thorough family assessment is necessary as part of the initial diagnostic evaluation of every child or adolescent with OCD. Family therapy is an important treatment consideration for pediatric OCD patients because family discord, marital difficulties, problems with a specific family member, or inappropriate roles or boundaries will interfere with the family's and the individual's functioning, and therefore will ultimately affect the long-term outcome of the identified patient (Hafner et al. 1981; Hoover and Insel 1984; Lenane 1991). Specific family therapy and/or marital therapy may be appropriate when family dysfunction or marital discord impedes OCD treatment. Lenane (1989) described the goals of family therapy as involving the whole family in treatment, getting all behaviors "out in the open," obtaining full and accurate understanding of how everyone in the family participates in the OCD behavior, and also reframing less-than-positive behavior. The end result of this process is that the family is better able to participate in the treatment plan of the identified OCD patient in a more positive and constructive manner.

Behavioral Treatment

Cognitive-behavior therapy (CBT)—in particular, in the form of exposure and response prevention (ERP)—has been well developed and studied in adults with OCD (Baer 1992; Foa and Emmelkamp 1983; Greist 1992; Marks 1987) but has not been systematically studied in children and adolescents with OCD. Original pediatric case reports suggested that behavioral techniques employed with adults (Marks 1987) were also appropriate for children (Berg et al. 1989; March et al. 1994; Wolfe and Wolfe 1991). CBT is used clinically with much success, although its efficacy is based predominantly on empirically supported and open trials (March 1995). Available reports suggest that techniques employed with adults (Marks 1987) are also generally applicable to and can be modified for children (for reviews, see Berg et al. 1989; March 1995; Wolff and Rapoport 1988; Wolfe and Wolfe 1991). In adults diagnosed with OCD, ERP is considered the behavior treatment of choice (Dar and Greist 1992). In the largest single pediatric behavioral study to date, Bolton and colleagues (1983) used ERP for 15 adolescents with OCD and achieved good treatment results in 11. In addition to ERP, other specific behavioral treatment techniques (e.g., anxiety management training and relaxation techniques) should be considered, with overall modification of these behavioral treatments for children (March et al. 1994).

There appears to be a shortage of mental health practitioners experienced in the behavioral treatment of OCD (March et al. 1994). Some clinicians may have misconceptions regarding CBT and ERP in children and adolescents with OCD, including those about time, effort, expense, and associated patient anxiety. Clinicians may complain that child patients do not comply with behavioral treatments, and parents may complain that clinicians are not specifically trained in CBT for OCD (March et al. 1994). The involvement of family members is paramount in the behavioral treatment of OCD. Familial overinvolvement, marital stress, and psychopathology can interfere with the success of behavior modification. There may be premature discontinuation of behavioral treatment.

Based on clinical reports, cognitive-behavioral psychotherapy, using ERP, appears to be an important behavioral treatment intervention to consider in children and adolescents with OCD. Exposure-based treatments include gradual (sometimes termed *graded*) exposure or flooding, with the exposure targets under patient and/or therapist control. For example, a child with contamination fears must come into and remain in contact with a particular OCD phobic stimulus. Dar and Greist (1992) have postulated that response prevention operates under the principle that adequate exposure depends on blocking rituals or avoidance behaviors. Thus, aside from touching "contaminated" objects, the patient must refrain from rituals to dispel the anxiety. Together, the patient and therapist develop a "tolerable" hierarchy of anxiety-producing stimuli, and these stimuli are assigned Subjective Units of Disturbance Scale (SUDS; Wolpe 1973) scores to quantify the increasing exposure. Through repeated exposure and response prevention, a substantial reduction eventually occurs in previously incapacitating anxiety on confrontation with the stimulus.

Other CBT techniques include anxiety management training, which consists of relaxation and breathing control training, and cognitive restructuring. Additional cognitive therapies are available (e.g., satiation, thought stopping, habit reversal) that may supplement ERP (for reviews, see March 1995; March et al. 1994). Habit reversal may play a role in the treatment of the more repetitive "complex tic-like rituals" (Vitulano et al. 1992).

Successful behavioral treatment of OCD requires developmental sensitivity and careful attention to unique issues in each age group. Children and adolescents with OCD may often view symptoms or experience distress and interference very differently from their parents (Berg et al. 1989). Thus, it is paramount for the CBT therapist to gain the child's cooperation, to individualize treatment, to attempt to instill in the child a sense of mastery and accomplishment, and to minimize massive initial anxiety (such as in flooding). Unlike CBT in adults with OCD, in which the therapist selects the treatment plan, hierarchy of exposure targets, and SUDS items, these tasks must be established by the child and therapist in collaboration. March and Mulle (1993) recently developed a protocol-driven treatment manual ("How I Ran OCD Off My Land") based on a framework of cognitive interventions and ERP (available on request from authors; see references). It is designed to facilitate patient and parental compliance, exportability to other clinicians, and empirical evaluation (March et al. 1994). For example, the child is in charge of choosing exposure targets and selecting metaphors. This manualized treatment protocol appears to be practical to implement and effective for treatment.

It should be reemphasized that empirical evidence for the efficacy of CBT in child subjects with OCD remains limited, especially in contrast to the literature on pharmacotherapy (Rapoport et al. 1992). March (1995) reviewed 32 investigations, most of them single case reports with varying degrees of terminology, theoretical framework, and methodological limitations (i.e., outcomes by self-report) and found that all but one found benefit for CBT interventions. Because most of these reports were not designed to test the specific effects of one behavioral protocol, it was difficult to draw generalizable conclusions. In most of these investigations, behavioral treatment was only one part of a multimodal approach and sometimes had only a secondary role. Future research in this area will use controlled trials—with standardized diagnostic definitions, baseline observations, established treatment time courses, and objective rating scales—and follow-up studies to compare medications, behavior therapy, and combination treatment (March 1995).

Several prognostic indicators for successful response to behavioral treatment of OCD include a motivated patient, the presence of overt rituals and compulsions, an ability to monitor and report symptoms, an absence of complicating comorbid illnesses, and a willingness to cooperate with treatment (Foa and Emmelkamp 1983). Behavior modification therapy may be less successful for patients with obsessions only (as opposed to both obsessions and compulsions), for very young patients, for uncooperative patients, or for those with obsessional slowness. Children with primary obsessional slowness generally respond poorly to both behavioral and medication treatment (Wolff and Rapoport 1988). Because ERP has not demonstrated significant benefit in obsessional slowness, modeling and shaping procedures may be the CBT treatment(s) of choice with this OCD subtype (Ratnasuriya et al. 1991). Future investigations with diverging subjects and clinical settings will be necessary to determine whether children and adolescents with difficult-to-manage OCD respond to manualized CBT.

Systematic comparisons of drug versus behavioral therapy in children and adolescents with OCD are limited, as are such studies in adults. There are few clinical guidelines for selecting initial treatment; thus, clinicians must carefully evaluate available behavioral treatments, patient cooperation, and constellation or specific symptom pattern. Baer and Minichiello (1990) suggest that medication and behavior therapy actually complement each other and that the use of antiobsessional agents may help improve compliance with behavioral treatment. Potential advantages of using behavioral therapy alone may include the avoidance of adverse medication side effects. March et al. (1994) hypothesized that booster behavior therapy may prevent relapse when medications are discontinued. Patients treated with medication and concurrent CBT (including booster treatments during medication discontinuation), as well as those for whom ongoing pharmacotherapy proves necessary, may exhibit both short- and long-term improvement in medication responsiveness (March 1995). In conclusion, CBT and pharmacotherapy appear to work well together, and many children with OCD require or would benefit from both CBT and pharmacotherapy (Piacentini et al. 1992).

Abundant clinical and emerging empirical evidence exists that CBT—alone or in combination with pharmacotherapy—is an important, safe, acceptable, and effective treatment for OCD in children and adolescents (March 1995; March et al. 1994). A proposed trial of CBT should be presented to and discussed with the child and family. As long as the patient is motivated and able to understand directions, he or she is an appropriate candidate for behavior treatment.

Pharmacological Treatment

SRIs such as clomipramine, fluoxetine, sertraline, and fluvoxamine have shown efficacy in controlled trials of adults with OCD (for a review, see March et al. 1995b). They may also prove to be effective treatments for children and adolescents with OCD. Early studies showed that children and adolescents with OCD responded well to the tricyclic antidepressant (TCA) and potent SRI clomipramine (Flament et al. 1985, 1988; Leonard et al. 1989). The first study consisted of 23 pediatric patients who participated in a 10-week double-blind, placebo-controlled crossover (Flament et al. 1985). Dosages of clomipramine targeting 3 mg/kg were used, with a mean dose of 141 mg/day. In the 19 OCD patients who completed the trial, clomipramine was significantly superior to placebo in decreasing obsessive-compulsive symptomatology at week 5, an improvement in symptoms could usually be seen as early as week 3, and 75% had moderate to marked improvement. In a large multicenter study, DeVeaugh-Geiss and colleagues (1992) reported that clomipramine was superior to placebo for the treatment of OCD in adolescents. This finding led to the U.S. Food and Drug Administration's (FDA) approval of clomipramine for the treatment of OCD in children and adolescents (10 years or older).

Clomipramine is unique among the TCAs in that it significantly inhibits serotonin reuptake. Its primary metabolite, desmethylclomipramine, is a potent noradrenergic reuptake inhibitor; thus, clomipramine has both noradrenergic and serotoninergic action. To assess the specificity of this agent, a double-blind, crossover comparison of clomipramine and desipramine (a selective noradrenergic-blocking TCA) was conducted in 48 children and adolescents with OCD (Leonard et al. 1989). Clomipramine was clearly superior to desipramine in ameliorating OCD symptoms at week 5, and some improvement could be seen as early as the third week of treatment. Desipramine was no more effective in improving obsessive-compulsive symptoms than placebo had been in the Flament and colleagues (1985) study. In fact, when desipramine was given as the second active medication, 64% of the patients had some degree of relapse within several weeks of crossover. Clomipramine was generally well tolerated in these studies, as it has been in clinical experience. Long-term clomipramine maintenance has not revealed any unexpected adverse reactions (DeVeaugh-Geiss et al. 1992; Leonard et al. 1991, 1995).

Anticholinergic, antihistaminic, and alpha-blocking side effects are associated with clomipramine. The most common side effects reported in children and adolescents include (in order of decreasing frequency) dry mouth, somnolence, dizziness, fatigue, tremor, headache, constipation, anorexia, abdominal pain, dyspepsia, and insomnia; these effects are comparable to (but anecdotally are reported as milder than) those reported in adults (DeVeaugh-Geiss et al. 1992; Leonard et al. 1989). Although no defined indications exist for electrocardiogram (ECG) or plasma-level monitoring, Leonard and colleagues (1995) suggest that baseline and periodic ECG monitoring are advisable. Several adolescents who discontinued clomipramine abruptly (during long-term maintenance) experienced withdrawal symptoms of gastrointestinal distress, which appeared to represent a cholinergic rebound syndrome, as has been reported with other antidepressants (Leonard et al. 1989). Thus, abrupt discontinuation of clomipramine is not recommended.

The SSRIs (e.g., fluoxetine, sertraline, paroxetine, fluvoxamine) are considered *selective* inhibitors of serotonin because of their limited effect on other monoamines (Warrington 1992). They represent a new class of agents with distinct advantages in their side-effect profiles and their broad therapeutic index over those of the TCAs. Riddle and colleagues (1990a, 1992) concluded that fluoxetine, FDA-approved for the treatment of depression and OCD in adults, appeared to be safe, effective, and well tolerated at dosages of 10–40 mg/day in children and adolescents with primary OCD or TS and OCD. Geller and colleagues (1995) found that fluoxetine may be effective in the treatment of OCD in prepubertal children and that the effect can be sustained over time. Dosages used in children may be as low as 5 mg/day. Fluoxetine and other SSRIs have less anticholinergic side effects than TCAs, but common side effects include nervousness, insomnia, activation, and restlessness. The majority of the side effects reported for SSRIs are from adult studies, and include complaints of nausea, headache, nervousness, insomnia, diarrhea, and drowsiness (Stokes 1993). The reader is referred to March and colleagues (1995a) for specific issues of dosage and monitoring in children and adolescents.

Systematic studies of the SSRIs are ongoing for the treatment of childhood and adolescent OCD. Evidence suggests that the drugs are well tolerated and effective. The advantage of the SSRIs' few anticholinergic side effects and limited cardiovascular toxicities are particularly relevant for the pediatric population (Leonard et al. 1995). The specific choice of SRI/SSRI should involve consideration of risk–benefit ratio, side-effect profile, pharmacokinetics (long versus short half-life), route of metabolism with other concomitant medications, comorbid diagnoses, and individual response (for a review of pediatric psychopharmacological treatment studies of OCD, see March and colleagues (1995a). Clinicians should inquire about all over-the-counter and recreational drugs and all prescription medications, especially terfenadine and astemizole (particularly in combination with certain medications; for example, ketoconazole), which have been shown to prolong the QT interval (Leonard et al. 1995). Additionally, it has been established that the combination of clomipramine and an SSRI may result in unexpectedly high clomipramine levels as a result of competitive inhibition by hepatic microenzyme systems.

Generally, a 12-week trial of an SRI/SSRI at an adequate dosage is considered necessary. Clinicians should be aware that many patients do not experience symptom relief until 6–10 weeks of receiving these agents, and that during early treatment (i.e., the first 1–10 days) with SSRIs, some patients may actually develop a worsening of their OCD symptoms or experience particularly annoying side effects (e.g., insomnia, increased psychomotor activity). This has been referred to as an "agitated syndrome" and has been well described in patients at certain doses and particularly in panic disorder patients. Typically, the exacerbation subsides and a positive clinical response ensues. Thus, the patient and the family should be educated and encouraged to report worsening or problematic side effects to the clinician. Initial worsening during the first week usually is not a reason in and of itself to discontinue the medication. For patients who exhibit a partial response to an SRI, augmentation strategies may be considered. Clonazepam is occasionally used, or a neuroleptic if a comorbid tic or schizotypal personality disorder is present (Leonard et al. 1994). Behavioral treatments should be considered as an adjunct to pharmacotherapy.

Many patients will continue to experience some OCD symptoms that vary ien severity over time, because of OCD's tendency to wax and wane. Although periodically decreasing the dosage should be considered, long-term maintenance may be required for some patients. Leonard and colleagues (1991) conducted a double-blind desipramine-substitution study of long-term clomipramine–maintained patients, and found that 8 of the 9 desipramine-substitution patients, but only 2 of the 11 nonsubstitution patients, relapsed. This result might argue for consideration of concomitant behavioral treatment. March and colleagues (1994) found greater improvement and lower relapse rates in patients treated with both medications and CBT. This issue clearly merits further study.

Although many patients respond early to one of the SRIs or SSRIs, a substantial minority do not respond until 8 or even 12 weeks of treatment (with therapeutic doses toward the end of this period). Thus, it is important for the clinician to be patient, to target a therapeutic dosage, and to wait at least 10–12 weeks before changing agents or undertaking augmentation regimens. If no clinical response has occurred after 12 weeks, switching to another SSRI would be reasonable.

Although various agents have been studied as augmentation strategies in adults and children with OCD, only clonazepam and haloperidol have been proven effective in controlled trials in adults (McDougle et al. 1994; Pigott and Rubenstein 1992). Clonazepam is a potential choice, but the clinician must also consider issues such as long-term dependency, cognitive effects, and possible side effects of paradoxical disinhibition. Thus, if only a partial response occurs after 12 weeks, the clinician might augment with clonazepam. Haloperidol should be used cautiously, and only if a comorbid tic-spectrum disorder or schizotypal personality disorder is present. A more systematic study of the use of augmentation medications in children and adolescents is indicated. Generally, augmentation strategies are started when there has been only a partial response to an SSRI, whereas an alternative SSRI is tried when there has been no response.

Summary

It is estimated that perhaps as many as 1 million children and adolescents in this country may have OCD. Childhood OCD presents in a form essentially identical to that seen in adults, and one-third of adult patients first developed the illness in childhood. Boys seem to have an earlier age at onset of OCD (prepuberty), whereas girls are more likely to develop OCD around puberty. Washing, repeating, checking, touching, counting, arranging, hoarding, and scrupulosity are the most commonly seen rituals. Almost all patients have reported a change in their principal symptoms over time. Increasing evidence supports a neurobiological theory for the etiology of OCD—specifically, a frontal lobe–basal ganglia dysfunction.

Most recent studies suggest that early (prepubertal)–occurring OCD and/or tic disorders characterized by abrupt onset and acute exacerbations may represent a subtype of pediatric OCD. Patients with this subtype typically have a comorbid tic disorder and an increased family loading. Identification of a new subtype of pediatric-onset OCD with abrupt onset and dramatic exacerbations may lead to new assessment and treatment interventions.

Childhood OCD and adult OCD appear to respond similarly to treatment. Although behavioral treatment has not been systematically studied in children and adolescents, reports suggest that ERP techniques are useful. In children and adolescents, clomipramine was superior to placebo and to desipramine at week 5 in a double-blind, crossover comparison (Leonard et al. 1989). Fluoxetine has been reported to be safe and well tolerated in the pediatric population, although systematic studies are still ongoing. Follow-up studies indicate that at least 50% of patients with pediatric-onset OCD are still symptomatic as adults (Berman 1942; Hollingsworth et al. 1980). These findings suggest that although the majority of OCD patients can expect improvement with the new treatments available, there remains a small group of patients who continue to have a chronic and debilitating course.

A number of important research issues exist for childhood-onset OCD. For example, it is not known which children will respond preferentially to behavioral or pharmacological treatments. The identification of children at risk for OCD, through genetic or biological studies, is a research priority. It is hoped that new treatment modalities and combinations of available treatments will improve the long-term outcome.

References

Ackerman D, Greenland S, Bystritsky A, et al: Predictors of treatment response in obsessive-compulsive disorder: multivariate analyses from a multicenter trial of clomipramine. J Clin Psychopharmacol 14:247–254, 1994

Allen AJ, Leonard HL, Swedo SE: Case study: a new infection-triggered, autoimmune subtype of pediatric OCD and Tourette's syndrome. Am Acad Child Adolesc Psychiatry 34:307–311, 1995

American Psychiatric Association: Diagnostic and Statistical Manual of Mental Disorders, 3rd Edition, Revised. Washington, DC, American Psychiatric Association, 1987

American Psychiatric Association: Diagnostic and Statistical Manual of Mental Disorders, 4th Edition. Washington, DC, American Psychiatric Association, 1994

Anderson JC, Williams S, McGee R, et al: DSM-III disorders in preadolescent children. Arch Gen Psychiatry 44:69–76, 1987

Baer L: Behavior therapy for obsessive-compulsive disorder and trichotillomania: implications for Tourette's syndrome. Adv Neurol 58:333–340, 1992

Baer L, Minichiello WE: Behavior therapy for obsessive-compulsive disorder, in Obsessive Compulsive Disorders: Theory and Management. Edited by Jenike M, Baer L, Minichiello W. Chicago, IL, Year Book Medical, 1990, pp 203–232

Berg CZ, Rapoport JL, Wolff RP: Behavioral treatment for obsessive-compulsive disorder in childhood, in Obsessive-Compulsive Disorder in Children and Adolescents. Edited by Rapoport JL. Washington, DC, American Psychiatric Press, 1989, pp 169–185

Berkowitz PH, Rothman EP: The Disturbed Child: Recognition and Psychoeducational Therapy in the Classroom. New York, New York University Press, 1960, pp 61–65

Berman L: Obsessive-compulsive neurosis in children. J Nerv Ment Dis 95:26–39, 1942

Black A: The natural history of obsessional neurosis, in Obsessional States. Edited by Beech HR. London, Methuen, 1974

Bolton D, Collins S, Steinberg D: The treatment of obsessive-compulsive disorder in adolescence: a report of fifteen cases. Br J Psychiatry 142:456–464, 1983

Cohen D, Leckman JF: Developmental psychopathology and neurobiology of Tourette's syndrome. J Am Acad Child Adolesc Psychiatry 33:2–15, 1994

Cox CS, Fedio P, Rapoport JL: Neuropsychological testing of obsessive compulsive adolescents, in Obsessive-Compulsive Disorder in Children and Adolescents. Edited by Rapoport JL. Washington, DC, American Psychiatric Press, 1989, pp 73–86

Cummings JL, Cunningham K: Obsessive-compulsive disorder in Huntington's disease. Biol Psychiatry 31:263–270, 1992

Dar R, Greist J: Behavior therapy for obsessive compulsive disorder. Psychiatr Clin North Am 15:885–894, 1992

Denckla MB: The neurological examination, in Obsessive-Compulsive Disorder in Children and Adolescents. Edited by Rapoport JL. Washington, DC, American Psychiatric Press, 1989, pp 107–118

DeVeaugh-Geiss GJ, Moroz G, Biederman J, et al: Clomipramine hydrochloride in childhood and adolescent obsessive-compulsive disorder: a multicenter trial. J Am Acad Child Adolesc Psychiatry 31:45–49, 1992

Esman A: Psychoanalysis in general psychiatry: obsessive-compulsive disorder as a paradigm. J Am Psychoanal Assoc 37:316–319, 1990

Flament MF, Rapoport JL, Berg C, et al: Clomipramine treatment of childhood obsessive-compulsive disorder. Arch Gen Psychiatry 42:977–983, 1985

Flament MF, Whitaker A, Rapoport JL, et al: Obsessive compulsive disorder in adolescence: an epidemiological study. J Am Acad Child Adolesc Psychiatry 27:764–771, 1988

Foa E, Emmelkamp P: Failures in Behavior Therapy. New York, Wiley & Sons, 1983

Frankel M, Cummings JL, Robertson MM, et al: Obsessions and compulsions in Gilles de la Tourette's syndrome. Neurology 36:378–382, 1986

Geller DA, Biederman J, Reed ED, et al: Similarities in response to fluoxetine in the treatment of children and adolescents with obsessive-compulsive disorder. J Am Acad Child Adolesc Psychiatry 34:36–44, 1995

Goodman WK, McDougle CJ, Price LH, et al: Beyond the serotonin hypothesis: a role for dopamine in some forms of obsessive compulsive disorder? J Clin Psychiatry 51 (suppl):36–43, 1990

Goodman WK, Price LH, Rasmussen SA, et al: The Yale-Brown Obsessive Compulsive Scale, Vol 2: Validity. Arch Gen Psychiatry 46:1012–1016, 1992

Greist JH: An integrated approach to treatment of obsessive compulsive disorder. J Clin Psychiatry 53 (suppl):38–41, 1992

Hafner RJ, Gilchrist P, Bowling J, et al: The treatment of obsessional neurosis in a family setting. Aust N Z J Psychiatry 15:145–151, 1981

Hanna GL: Demographic and clinical features of obsessive-compulsive disorder in children and adolescents. J Am Acad Child Adolesc Psychiatry 34:19–27, 1995

Hollingsworth C, Tanguay P, Grossman L, et al: Long-term outcome of obsessive compulsive disorder in childhood. J Am Acad Child Psychiatry 19:134–144, 1980

Holzer JC, Goodman WK, McDougle CJ, et al: Obsessive-compulsive disorder with and without a chronic tic disorder: a comparison of symptoms in 70 patients. Br J Psychiatry 164:469–473, 1994

Hoover CF, Insel TR: Families of origin in obsessive compulsive disorder. J Nerv Ment Dis 172:207–215, 1984

Insel TR: Toward a neuroanatomy of obsessive-compulsive disorder. Arch Gen Psychiatry 49:739–744, 1992

Jenike MA: Psychotherapy of Obsessive-Compulsive Personality Disorder. Chicago, IL, Year Book Medical, 1990

Judd LL: Obsessive compulsive neurosis in children. Arch Gen Psychiatry 12:136–143, 1965

Karno B, Golding J, Sorenson S, et al: The epidemiology of obsessive compulsive disorder in five U.S. communities. Arch Gen Psychiatry 45:1094–1099, 1988

King RA: Practice parameters for the psychiatric assessment of children and adolescents. J Am Acad Child Adolesc Psychiatry 34:1386–1402, 1995

Last CG, Strauss CC: Obsessive-compulsive disorder in childhood. Journal of Anxiety Disorders 3:295–302, 1989

Leckman JF, Walker DE, Cohen DJ: Premonitory urges in Tourette's Syndrome. Am J Psychiatry 150:98–102, 1993

Leckman JF, Walker DE, Goodman WK, et al: Just right perceptions associated with compulsive behavior in Tourette's syndrome. Am J Psychiatry 151:675–680, 1994

Lenane M: Families and obsessive-compulsive disorder, in Obsessive-Compulsive Disorder in Children and Adolescents. Edited by Rapoport JL. Washington, DC, American Psychiatric Press, 1989, pp 237–252

Lenane M: Family therapy for children with obsessive compulsive disorder, in Current Treatments of Obsessive-Compulsive Disorder. Edited by Pato MT, Zohar M. Washington, DC, American Psychiatric Press, 1991, pp 103–113

Lenane M, Swedo S, Leonard H, et al: Psychiatric disorders in first degree relatives of children and adolescents with obsessive compulsive disorder. J Am Acad Child Adolesc Psychiatry 29:407–412, 1990

Leonard HL, Swedo S, Rapoport JL, et al: Treatment of obsessive compulsive disorder with clomipramine and desipramine in children and adolescents: a double-blind crossover comparison. Arch Gen Psychiatry 46:1088–1092, 1989

Leonard HL, Swedo SE, Lenane MC, et al: A double-blind desipramine substitution during long-term clomipramine treatment in children and adolescents with obsessive-compulsive disorder. Arch Gen Psychiatry 48:922–926, 1991

Leonard HL, Lenane MC, Swedo SE, et al: Tics and Tourette's syndrome: a 2- to 7-year follow-up study of 54 obsessive-compulsive children. Am J Psychiatry 149:1244–1251, 1992

Leonard HL, Topol D, Bukstein O, et al: Clonazepam as an augmenting agent in the treatment of childhood-onset obsessive-compulsive disorder. J Am Acad Child Adolesc Psychiatry 33:792–794, 1994

Leonard H, Swedo S, March J, et al: Obsessive-compulsive disorder, in Treatments of Psychiatric Disorders, 2nd Edition. Edited by Gabbard G. Washington, DC, American Psychiatric Press, 1995, pp 301–313

Luxenberg JS, Swedo SE, Flament MF, et al: Neuroanatomical abnormalities in obsessive-compulsive disorder detected with quantitative X-ray computed tomography. Am J Psychiatry 145:1089–1093, 1988

March J: Cognitive-behavioral psychotherapy for children and adolescents with OCD: a review and recommendations for treatment. J Am Acad Child Adolesc Psychiatry 34:7–18, 1995

March J, Mulle K: How I ran OCD off my land: a cognitive-behavioral program for the treatment of obsessive-compulsive disorder in children and adolescents. Durham, NC, Duke University, Department of Child Psychiatry, 1993[1]

---

[1] Available from the Obsessive-Compulsive Foundation (OCF), P.O. Box 70, Milford, CT 06460; (203) 878-5669.

March J, Mulle K, Herbel B: Behavioral psychotherapy for children and adolescents with obsessive-compulsive disorder: an open trial of a new protocol-driven treatment package. J Am Acad Child Adolesc Psychiatry 33:333–341, 1994

March J, Leonard HL, Swedo SE: Obsessive compulsive disorder, in Anxiety Disorders in Children and Adolescents. Edited by March J. New York, Guilford, 1995a, pp 251–275

March JS, Leonard HL, Swedo SE: Pharmacotherapy of obsessive-compulsive disorder. Child Adolesc Psychiatr Clin North Am 4:217–236, 1995b

Marks IM: Fears, Phobias and Rituals, Panic Anxiety and Their Disorders. Oxford, England, Oxford University Press, 1987

McDougle C, Goodman W, Leckman JJ, et al: Haloperidol addition in fluvoxamine-refractory obsessive compulsive disorder. Arch Gen Psychiatry 51:302–308, 1994

Pauls DL, Towbin K, Leckman J, et al: Gilles de la Tourette syndrome and obsessive-compulsive disorder: evidence supporting a genetic relationship. Arch Gen Psychiatry 43:1180–1182, 1986

Pauls DL, Alsobrook JP, Goodman W, et al: A family study of obsessive-compulsive disorder. Am J Psychiatry 152:76–84, 1995

Piacentini J, Jaffer M, Gitow A, et al: Psychopharmacologic treatment of child and adolescent obsessive compulsive disorder. Psychiatr Clin North Am 15:87–107, 1992

Pigott T, Rubenstein C: A controlled trial of clonazepam augmentation in OCD patients treated with clomipramine or fluoxetine. Paper presented at the 145th Annual Meeting of the American Psychiatric Association, Washington, DC, May 2–7, 1992

Rapoport JL: Annotation: child obsessive-compulsive disorder. J Child Psychol Psychiatry 27:285–289, 1986

Rapoport JL (ed): Obsessive-Compulsive Disorder in Children and Adolescents. Washington, DC, American Psychiatric Press, 1989

Rapoport J, Swedo S, Leonard H: Childhood obsessive compulsive disorder. J Clin Psychiatry 53 (suppl):6–11, 1992

Ratnasuriya R, Marks IM, Forshaw D, et al: Obsessional slowness revisited. Br J Psychiatry 159:273–274, 1991

Rettew DC, Swedo SE, Leonard HL, et al: Obsessions and compulsions across time in 79 children and adolescents with obsessive compulsive disorder. J Am Acad Child Adolesc Psychiatry 29:766–772, 1992

Riddle MA, Hardin M, King R, et al: Fluoxetine treatment of children and adolescents with Tourette's and obsessive compulsive disorders: preliminary clinical experience. J Am Acad Child Adolesc Psychiatry 29:45–48, 1990a

Riddle MA, Scahill L, King R, et al: Obsessive compulsive disorder in children and adolescents: phenomenology and family history. J Am Acad Child Adolesc Psychiatry 29:766–772, 1990b

Riddle MA, Scahill L, King R, et al: Double-blind, crossover trial of fluoxetine and placebo in children and adolescents with obsessive-compulsive disorder. J Am Acad Child Adolesc Psychiatry 31:1062–1069, 1992

Rutter M, Tizard J, Whitmore K: Education, Health and Behavior. London, Longmans, 1970

Stokes PE: Fluoxetine: a five-year review. Clin Ther 15:216–243, 1993

Swedo SE: Sydenham's chorea: a model for childhood autoimmune neuropsychiatric disorders. JAMA 272:1788–1791, 1994

Swedo SE, Rapoport JL: Phenomenology and differential diagnosis of obsessive-compulsive disorder in children and adolescents, in Obsessive-Compulsive Disorder in Children and Adolescents. Edited by Rapoport JL. Washington, DC, American Psychiatric Press, 1989, pp 13–33

Swedo SE, Rapoport JL, Cheslow DL, et al: High prevalence of obsessive-compulsive symptoms in patients with Sydenham's chorea. Am J Psychiatry 146:246–249, 1989a

Swedo SE, Rapoport JL, Leonard HL, et al: Obsessive-compulsive disorder in children and adolescents: clinical phenomenology of 70 consecutive cases. Arch Gen Psychiatry 46:335–344, 1989b

Swedo SE, Shapiro ME, Grady CL, et al: Cerebral glucose metabolism in childhood-onset obsessive compulsive disorder. Arch Gen Psychiatry 46:518–523, 1989c

Swedo SE, Pietrini P, Leonard HL, et al: Cerebral glucose metabolism in childhood-onset obsessive-compulsive disorder. Arch Gen Psychiatry 49:690–694, 1992

Swedo SE, Leonard HL, Schapiro MB, et al: Sydenham's chorea: physical and psychological symptoms of St. Vitus's Dance. Pediatrics 91:706–713, 1993

Swedo SE, Leonard HL, Kiessling LS: Speculations on antineuronal antibody-mediated neuropsychiatric disorders of childhood: commentaries. Pediatrics 93:323–326, 1994

Vitulano LA, King RA, Scahill L, et al. Behavioral treatment of children and adolescents with trichotillomania. J Am Acad Child Adolesc Psychiatry 31:139–146, 1992

Von Economo C: Encephalitis Lethargica: Its Sequelae and Treatment. Translated by Neuman KO. New York, Oxford University Press, 1931

Walkup JT, LaBuda MJ, Hurko O, et al: Evidence for a mixed model of inheritance in Tourette's syndrome. Paper presented at the 42nd Annual Meeting of the American Academy of Child and Adolescent Psychiatry, New Orleans, LA, October 21, 1995

Warrington SJ: Clinical implications of the pharmacology of serotonin reuptake inhibitors. Int Clin Psychopharmacol 7:13–19, 1992

Wise SP, Rapoport JL: Obsessive-compulsive disorder: is it basal ganglia dysfunction? in Obsessive Compulsive Disorder in Children and Adolescents. Edited by Rapoport JL. Washington, DC, American Psychiatric Press, 1989, pp 327–344

Wolff R, Rapoport JL: Behavioral treatment of childhood obsessive compulsive disorder. Behav Modif 12:252–266, 1988

Wolfe RP, Wolfe LS: Assessment and treatment of obsessive-compulsive disorder in children. Behav Modif 15:372–393, 1991

Wolpe J: The Practice of Behavior Therapy, 2nd Edition. New York, Pergamon, 1973

Chapter 12

Obsessive-Compulsive Disorder in Adults

Michele T. Pato, M.D., and Carlos N. Pato, M.D.

Clinical Characteristics

Although obsessive-compulsive disorder (OCD) has finally been recognized as an important illness in childhood, there are still a large number of individuals with OCD who do not experience significant symptoms until adulthood. However, as we look at the symptoms of OCD throughout the life cycle, it is important to note that patients are usually stricken at a relatively young age even in adulthood, with a mean age at onset of 19.8 ± 9.6 years, and that fewer than 15% of patients date the onset of their symptoms after age 35 (Rasmussen and Eisen 1991).

Clinically, patients with OCD present with many different types of obsessions and compulsions. The symptom checklist of the Yale-Brown Obsessive Compulsive Scale (Y-BOCS; Goodman et al. 1989b) is one of the most clinically useful methods for assessing OCD. The value of elucidating the specific obsessions and compulsions with which a patient presents is twofold. First, given the secretive nature of and the sense of embarrassment many patients feel about their symptoms, the act of divulging these symptoms to the clinician often represents a critical step in the establishment of clinician-patient rapport—one that will ultimately affect patient compliance. Second, the identification of specific symptoms is important for the designing of individualized treatment. In the case of behavioral therapy in particular, the challenges and hierarchies developed must be specifically related to the symptoms present.

Obsessions are usually described as recurrent, intrusive, unwanted ideas. They often consist of disturbing thoughts or impulses that are difficult to dismiss. Compulsions are behaviors that are often, but not always, repetitive and can be either observable or mental. The compulsive behaviors are intended to reduce the anxiety engendered by obsessions. Many people, even those without OCD, may perform certain behaviors in a ritualistic way, repeating, checking, or washing things over and over out of habit or concern. What distinguishes OCD as a psychiatric disorder is that the experience of obsessions, and the performance of rituals, reaches such an intensity or frequency that it causes significant psychological distress or interferes in a significant way with psychosocial functioning. The guideline of at least 1 hour expended on symptoms per day (American Psychiatric Association 1994; Goodman et al. 1989b) has been presented as a measure for "significant interference." However, in patients who often avoid situations that bring on rituals, the actual symptoms may not consume an hour, yet the amount of "time lost" from having to avoid objects or situations would surely be defined as interfering with functioning. Consider, for instance, the single mother of three on welfare who throws out more than $100 of groceries a week because of contamination fears. Although such behavior surely has an impact on socioeconomic functioning, one may be hard pressed to demonstrate that it consumes 1 hour per day.

Historically, individuals with OCD were distinguished from those with psychotic disorders by the maintenance of insight into the irrational and senseless nature of their symptoms. However, as more and more patients have sought treatment and more careful longitudinal assessments have been conducted, it has become apparent that patients can exhibit a full range of insight about their symptoms, from complete awareness (excellent insight) to delusional insight (poor insight) (Eisen and Rasmussen 1993; Foa and Kozak 1995; Insel and Akiskal 1986; Kozak and Foa 1994; Lelliott et al. 1988). Given this clearer clinical picture of OCD, DSM-IV (American Psychiatric Association 1994), unlike previous DSM editions, includes a new specifier for OCD: "with poor insight." Such specification is important because this factor seems to have some bearing on treatment choice and outcome (Foa 1979). Specifically, patients with poor insight that reaches psychotic proportions can have comorbid schizoid or schizotypal personality disorder or schizophrenia and tend to be more treatment resistant. These psychotic or delusional patients may benefit from the addition of an antipsychotic medication (Eisen and Rasmussen 1993; McDougle et al. 1990).

The typical pattern for obsessions and compulsions is for the obsessions to cause a mounting sense of anxiety or concern that can be nullified only by either performing a compulsion or avoiding the situation that brings on the obsessional thinking. Thus, the obsessions and compulsions often occur together—for example, obsessional fear of dirt, germs, or contaminants leading to excessive washing of hands, sanitizing of objects, or avoidance of touching anything that might be contaminated. Based on the DSM-IV field trials, the most common obsessions are contamination and fear of harming oneself or others. The most common compulsions are checking and cleaning/washing (Foa and Kozak 1995). The presence of obsessions without compulsions is rare. Often, adult patients who appear to have only obsessions actually have subtle compulsions such as repeated asking for reassurance that they did something correctly or that something did happen. Others may have difficult-to-observe mental rituals such as counting in their head or saying things over and over again, be it a prayer, a nonsense phrase, or a short rhyme. The presence of compulsions without obsessions also appears to be quite rare but has been noted in young children 6–8 years of age (Swedo et al. 1989a). One is left to wonder whether some obsessions have evolved as a way of rationalizing the irrational compulsive behaviors that OCD patients feel driven to perform.

Some typical examples of such obsession/compulsion pairs are described below. Contamination fears are usually characterized by a fear of dirt or germs but may also involve toxins or environmental hazards (e.g., asbestos, lead) or bodily waste or secretions. Patients usually describe a fear that harm will come to them or others by contact with the feared contaminants. For instance, a 33-year-old mother of a 5-year-old would not allow her son outside to play if she saw a Chemlawn truck on the street, fearing that he might somehow become contaminated. As her symptoms evolved, she could no longer buy groceries except in an organic supermarket because of her fear of chemical contaminants. Eventually, she stopped cooking for her family completely, forcing them to go for meals to relatives, out of fear she could not prepare food that was not contaminated. Another middle-aged woman with Crohn's disease spent hours in the shower washing herself in a special sequence and needed to have her adolescent children available to hand her a towel directly from the dryer to ensure that it had not been contaminated by touching the towel rack or floor of the bathroom.

Pathological doubt and compulsions such as checking, counting, and asking for reassurance is another obsessive-compulsive pairing often seen in OCD patients. Patients with pathological doubt are often concerned that as a result of their carelessness, harm will come to themselves or someone else. This concern has often been described as a "sense of overresponsibility." Patients with these symptoms often tend to "catastrophize," or see the worst possible outcome, no matter how unlikely. Often, OCD patients with these symptoms find it difficult to take medications. Not only is it hard for them to take risks or to feel out of control, but they are also convinced that they will experience every side effect, no matter how rare. This pathological doubt may lead to compulsive avoidance to the point of being housebound. Such a presentation can be difficult to distinguish from severe agoraphobia. A careful history will usually reveal that the avoidance is precipitated by obsessive thoughts rather than a fear of open spaces, crowds, or panic attacks.

Pathological doubt can also appear in conjunction with aggressive obsessions that are often described as a fear of doing violent harm to others. For instance, an adoring aunt refused to babysit her nieces and nephews, fearing that she might take a knife and stab them while they were sleeping. A man in his 40s could not take the subway to work for fear that he would act on his obsessive thought of pushing someone off the platform into an oncoming train. No amount of reassurance that they were not violent people by nature could convince these patients that they would not do these things. However, through behavioral therapy with exposure and response prevention (ERP), which included not avoiding these situations, the obsessive thoughts and the compulsive avoidance were treated.

Somatic obsessions are worries that one will contract or has contracted an illness or disease. Common somatic obsessions include a fear of cancer, venereal disease, or acquired immunodeficiency syndrome (AIDS). Checking compulsions consisting of checking and rechecking the body part of concern, as well as reassurance seeking, are commonly associated with this fear. The difference between the somatic obsessions of OCD and the somatic obsessions of hypochondriasis may be unclear, but there are several distinguishing features. Patients with OCD usually have a history of other "classic" OCD obsessions (e.g., checking, reassurance seeking). They are more likely to engage in these classic OCD compulsions and may not experience somatic symptoms of illness.

Comorbidity and Differential Diagnosis

It is sometimes difficult to determine, on the basis of a single symptom, whether the problem requiring treatment is OCD or another disorder. At times, a symptom may be shared by a number of different disorders, thus making it difficult to perform a differential diagnosis. At other times, the symptom may be shared by OCD and another comorbid disorder. Nonetheless, this distinction between a comorbid disorder with OCD and a distinct disorder that is not OCD can have a significant bearing on treatment decisions, as the following example illustrates. Patient 1, a young man who presents with a swinging of his glance from side to side in what looked like a motor tic, may on further questioning report that the entire behavior was motivated by a need for symmetry (diagnosis: OCD). Patient 2, another young man demonstrating the same motor behavior, might describe a motor tic to the right with a compulsion to the left to balance out the behavior symmetrically (diagnosis: OCD and tic disorder). Finally, patient 3 may have no explanation at all for his motor behavior other than an involuntary urge to perform it (diagnosis: tic disorder). Treatment of these three patients would vary, with patient 1 receiving a selective serotonin reuptake inhibitor (SSRI), patient 2 receiving both an SSRI and a high-potency neuroleptic (e.g., haloperidol, pimozide), and patient 3 receiving haloperidol or pimozide alone.

Tourette's syndrome and complex motor tics are often comorbid with OCD. Other potentially comorbid disorders include psychotic disorders (especially when insight is an issue), major depression (especially with excessive rumination), other anxiety disorders (specific phobias, social phobia, agoraphobia), hypochondriasis, body dysmorphic disorder, impulse-control disorder, and obsessive-compulsive personality disorder. In trying to differentiate among potential alternative diagnoses, it is often helpful to consider content of the person's thoughts (obsessions) or behaviors (compulsions). If the content is limited in its focus—for instance, a concern about the hopelessness of life (as in depressive ruminations), about bodily appearance (as in body dysmorphic disorder), about pulling hair (as in trichotillomania, an impulse-control disorder), or about thinness and food (as in anorexia nervosa), it is better to diagnose and treat these disorders. However, if these more focused symptoms appear along with more typical obsessions and compulsions and cause significant functional impairment and distress, a diagnosis of OCD may be more appropriate. Finally, in cases in which two distinct illnesses are present that seem to have different severity and/or different time courses or responses to treatment, comorbid disorders should be diagnosed and treated. For instance, there is a relatively high comorbidity between anorexia nervosa and OCD (Rubenstein et al. 1992). In one study, 17% of 100 OCD subjects were found to have a lifetime history of an eating disorder (Rasmussen and Eisen 1991). In another series of 93 subjects with an eating disorder, 37% met criteria for comorbid OCD (Thiel et al. 1995).

OCD and Other Anxiety Disorders

In DSM-IV, OCD is classified as an anxiety disorder because of the features it shares with other anxiety disorders—namely, the evocation of anxiety and the management of anxiety by means of avoidance. At times, patients will present complaining of a specific "phobia" such as "I'm phobic about dirt." At first glance, this complaint might appear to represent a simple phobia, in which patients avoid anything dirty, use gloves, and experience extreme anxiety or even panic attacks if they feel they have dirt on them. However, on further exploration, the clinician may find that the symptoms are based on contamination concerns and might even involve rituals or ritualistic avoidance of certain objects or things. Examples may include never entering certain rooms in the house or touching certain objects without using a tissue. In such cases, OCD may be a more accurate diagnosis.

A critical distinction must be made with respect to treatment, given that the treatment of panic disorder is relatively nonspecific, making use of a number of different antidepressants and benzodiazepines. In contrast, the treatment of OCD is quite specific, and a SSRI is commonly indicated. This specificity in treatment has prompted some to argue against including OCD as an anxiety disorder. The European symptom classification (International Classification of Diseases, 10th Revision [ICD-10; World Health Organization 1992]) does not classify OCD as an anxiety disorder, but instead places it in a separate group (Montgomery

1994). Anxiety disorders frequently coexist with OCD. Relatively high lifetime rates of social phobia (18%), panic disorder (12%), and specific phobia (22%) are reported in patients with OCD (Rasmussen and Eisen 1991).

OCD and Body Dysmorphic Disorder

Like patients with OCD, patients with body dysmorphic disorder (BDD) can experience obsessional thinking around their supposed defect in appearance and will often engage in rituals such as mirror checking, reassurance seeking, and avoidance (Phillips 1991). In addition, the existing data seem to indicate that, as in OCD, SSRIs have some treatment efficacy in BDD (Phillips et al. 1995). Although more data are needed on differentiating these two disorders, if obsessions and compulsions concern only bodily appearance, a diagnosis of BDD should be made. However, if obsessions and compulsions unrelated to appearance issues are also present, the OCD diagnosis should be given.

OCD and Tourette's Syndrome

There is compelling evidence of the relationship between Tourette's syndrome (TS) and OCD. Of particular note is that 7% of OCD patients also meet criteria for TS (Rasmussen and Eisen 1991), and patients with TS have a high rate of OCD symptoms. The combined prevalence of TS symptoms plus OCD is about 30%–40% (Lees et al. 1984; Robertson et al. 1988). Differentiating the intrusive urge to perform a tic from an obsessional drive to perform a compulsion is not always easy. The patient will often describe a muscle tension or a physical urge rather than the obsessional thought and anxiety that precede compulsive motor behaviors. Most important, then, is the patient's explanation about why he or she performs the behavior.

OCD Versus Obsessive-Compulsive Personality Disorder

Research on the coexistence of OCD and personality disorders has been hampered by some methodological concerns, including relatively poor interrater reliability for Axis II disorders. In a study of 96 subjects with OCD in which a structured interview with adequate interrater reliability (the Structured Interview for DSM-III Personality Disorders [SID-P; Stangl et al. 1985]) was used, 36% met criteria for one or more DSM-III (American Psychiatric Association 1984) personality disorders (Baer et al. 1990). Dependent (12%), histrionic (9%), and obsessive-compulsive (6%) personality disorders were diagnosed most frequently, but other comorbid personality disorders (schizotypal [5%], paranoid [5%], and avoidant [5%]) were also noted. A higher rate of obsessive-compulsive personality disorder (OCPD) was found with DSM-III-R (American Psychiatric Association 1987) criteria (25% of 59 OCD probands), which may reflect changes in the criteria set between DSM-III and DSM-III-R. The comorbidity of OCD and OCPD appears relatively low, a finding that is at odds with earlier literature, which postulated that OCD and OCPD are closely related disorders on a continuum of severity. Although personality disorders are considered to be stable over time, a recent study found that among 17 OCD patients with a personality disorder, 9 of 10 treatment responders no longer met criteria for a personality disorder after successful pharmacotherapy, thus raising the question of whether the apparent personality disorder was actually a manifestation of, or a result of, chronic OCD (Ricciardi et al. 1992).

OCD Versus Psychotic and Impulse-Control Disorders

Although it is easy to provide specific examples of obsessions and compulsions that help to distinguish them from other behaviors that might be part of a more psychotic picture or an impulse-control disorder, in real life these distinctions are often hard to make. It may be preferable to think of the mental phenomena of obsessions on a continuum from normal worry to ruminations to overvalued ideas and delusions. In addition, OCD patients rarely stay in one place along this continuum. Eisen and Rasmussen (1993) and Insel and Akiskal (1986) have noted that individuals with OCD can develop a transient delusional certainty about their thoughts or rituals. In a similar vein, how can one explain behaviors as varied as compulsive gambling or shopping, hair pulling, and hand washing over which a patient feels little control yet is compelled to perform? One framework that has been offered to deal with this broad spectrum of thoughts and behaviors posits continua along the dimensions of "uncertainty–certainty" and "risk aversion–risk seeking" (Hollander 1993). In such a framework, patients with OCD occupy a position at the uncertainty and the risk-avoidance ends of the continua—often ridden with doubt about the need to perform their rituals, yet uncertain enough about the risk of harm that "to be safe," they ritualize. Within such a framework, a whole spectrum of disorders that share some common features (e.g., clinical symptoms, family history, comorbidity, genetic transmission, treatment response, etiology) can be viewed as related. These "OC-related disorders" include BDD, depersonalization disorder, anorexia nervosa, hypochondriasis, trichotillomania, TS, sexual compulsions, pathological gambling, impulse-control disorders, and delusional disorders.

Etiology and Pathophysiology

The evidence regarding the etiology and pathophysiology of OCD is by no means definitive. Factors contributing to OCD can be broadly categorized into neurochemical, neuroanatomical, neuroimmunological, genetic, ethological, learning theory, and psychodynamic.

Neurochemical Contributions

Serotonin plays an important role but does not appear to be the sole factor involved in OCD. Exploration of the role of serotonin in OCD is based on three types of studies: 1) direct measurements of concentrations of central and peripheral neurotransmitters and their metabolites, 2) pharmacological challenge studies measuring the immediate behavioral and neuroendocrinological effects of certain pharmacological agents, and 3) treatment trials measuring the response of patients to chronic administration of medications that differentially affect specific neurotransmitters (Pigott 1996). To date, the most consistent data supporting the serotonin hypothesis have come from treatment trials. More specifically, the most effective agents all seem to be serotonin reuptake inhibitors. Treatment trials with drugs having other 5-hydroxytryptamine (5-HT) mechanisms of action (trazodone and *m*-chlorophenylpiperazine [m-CPP]) have not been effective (Pigott et al. 1992b). A correlation between relative affinity for reuptake sites and relative efficacy has not been borne out. Such a correlation would imply that fluvoxamine would have the greatest antiobsessional effect, since it is the most potent inhibitor of reuptake, followed by sertraline, paroxetine, fluoxetine, and clomipramine. However, clomipramine may be superior to the more selective agents, which are probably about equal in efficacy (DeVane 1992; Greist et al. 1995c; Pigott 1996). (See "Treatment" section for more details.)

Findings from direct measurement of cerebrospinal 5-hydroxyindoleacetic acid (5-HIAA) (Thorén et al. 1980) and platelet serotonin levels (Flament et al. 1987) have not always been consistent but have supported the notion that perturbations in the serotonin system are more common in OCD patients than in control subjects. Similarly, challenge studies with agents that specifically affect the functional integrity of the serotonin system, such as tryptophan (Barr et al. 1994), fenfluramine (Hewlett and Martin 1993), metergoline (Pigott et al. 1991), and m-CPP (Hollander et al. 1992; Zohar et al. 1987), have at times suggested that serotonergic—but not dopaminergic or adrenergic—dysregulation plays the major role in OCD (for a review, see Pigott 1996).

In an attempt to further explore the neurochemistry of OCD and how it relates to the serotonin system, studies have measured serum metabolites of various effective medications. Again, results have been unhelpful in that most studies have not identified any specific correlation between serum levels of parent compounds or metabolites and overall efficacy (Flament et al. 1987; Insel et al. 1983; Thorén et al. 1980). However, one study (Mavissakalian et al. 1990) has provided at least some support for the serotonin hypothesis. In this study, the concentration of the serotonergic parent compound clomipramine, but not of its noradrenergic metabolite *N*-desmethylclomipramine, correlated positively with symptom improvement. Compared with nonresponders, responders tended to have higher clomipramine levels and lower ratios of N-desmethylclomipramine to clomipramine (Mavissakalian et al. 1990).

Augmentation studies with dopamine antagonists such as haloperidol, pimozide, and, most recently, risperidone (Jacobsen 1995) in patients with comorbid tics and psychotic symptoms have contributed to the belief that the dopamine system may also be involved in the pathophysiology of OCD (Goodman et al. 1990). Neuroimmunological factors may also play a role (see Chapter 11 in this volume). However, despite the many pharmacological manipulations conducted, the interplay among the various neurotransmitters, their contribution to the etiology of OCD, and their implications for treatment of the illness remain unclear.

Neuroanatomical Contributions

Anecdotal and historical evidence of insults to basal ganglion structures leading to OCD had already implicated these structures in the etiology of the disorder (Insel 1992; Insel and Winslow 1992). However, some of the most compelling work comes from brain-imaging studies. Various imaging techniques have been used, including static measures such as computed tomography (CT) as well as functional measures such as positron-emission tomography (PET) and functional magnetic resonance imaging (MRI). The latter techniques have been particularly exciting because they afford the investigator the opportunity to "watch" the obsessions evolve in the brain as the patient in the scanner is "challenged" with stimuli that bring on his or her obsessions and compulsions (Rauch et al. 1994). These various techniques have implicated areas of the brain that—not surprisingly—are often rich in serotonin connections and, in addition, seem to play a role in behaviors related to process and procedural learning and approach and avoidance behaviors (Schwartz et al. 1996). More specifically, PET studies have shown increased glucose metabolism in the caudate nucleus and orbitofrontal cortex in untreated OCD patients compared with control subjects (Baxter et al. 1988; Nordahl et al. 1989; Swedo et al. 1989b). When the OCD patients were challenged with feared stimuli, changes in the caudate, cingulate cortex, and orbitofrontal cortex were noted (Rauch et al. 1994). Studies comparing PET scans pre- and posttreatment showed a correlation between treatment response and normalization of the increased activity of the caudate nucleus (Baxter et al. 1992; Benkelfat et al. 1990; Hoehn-Saric et al. 1991; Schwartz et al. 1996; Swedo et al. 1992).

Genetic Contributions

The two basic approaches that have been used to explore genetic factors in OCD have been twin studies and family studies. Twin studies have revealed a concordance rate among monozygotic twins of 63%. This finding obviously supports a genetic contribution to OCD but is not the 100% concordance that one would expect in a simple dominantly inherited disorder (Rasmussen and Tsuang 1986).

The family-study work has also lent support to a genetic component in the transmission of OCD. Whereas early studies had indicated increased frequencies of OCD in families (McKeon and Murray 1987), the most accurate data come from more recent studies (Black et al. 1992; Lenane et al. 1990; Pauls et al. 1995; Riddle et al. 1990) that have used more rigorous methodologies, including structured interviews, systematic diagnostic criteria, control groups, and direct interviews of relatives. In the Pauls et al. (1995) study, which included 100 OCD patients and direct interviews with 446 first-degree relatives, 10.3% of the relatives met criteria for OCD and an additional 7.9% had "subthreshold" OCD. This represented a significantly higher rate than that found in a comparison control group in which 1.9% of relatives had OCD and 2.0% of relatives had subthreshold OCD. In another family study, age at onset was shown to have some significance, with an increased frequency of OCD within the family when the patient's age at onset was younger than 14 years (Bellodi et al. 1992).

Given the comorbidity between TS and OCD, it is not surprising that family studies of TS have also contributed to the supporting data on a role for genetics in OCD. First-degree relatives of patients with TS had a much higher rate of OCD as well as tics and TS. The overall risk was higher for males than for females; in addition, females were more likely to have OCD and males to have tics or TS (Pauls et al. 1991). In terms of OCD prevalence among first-degree relatives, 13% had OCD alone and 10% had OCD and tics or TS, for a total of 23% with OCD (Pauls et al. 1986). These rates of OCD are much higher than the approximate 2% prevalence of OCD that has been found in epidemiological studies (Robins et al. 1984). The child literature also supports increased frequencies of TS and tics among first-degree relatives in child patients with OCD (Leonard et al. 1992).

Ethological (Animal) Contributions

One of the more compelling animal models is a kind of compulsive grooming behavior seen in dogs, called *canine acral lick syndrome*. In this condition, dogs (and cats) cause cutaneous lesions to the skin and hair loss secondary to excessive grooming (Rapoport et al. 1992). Interestingly, not only does the condition worsen with stress, but it has been treated successfully with the same serotonin reuptake inhibitors used in OCD: clomipramine, fluoxetine, and sertraline. However, other animal models have not been so straightforward. Many of the repetitive and grooming animal behaviors that are likened to compulsions seen in OCD seem to be precipitated or exacerbated by drugs that manipulate the dopamine rather than the serotonin system (Pitman 1991).

Learning Theory Contributions

The contributions of learning theory to understanding OCD have been more in the area of how the symptoms are perpetuated than in how they actually arise. However, this understanding has allowed for important breakthroughs in developing effective nonpharmacological treatments. The underlying tenets of learning theory regarding OCD are based on a model of conditioning, tension reduction, and lack of habituation. According to the theory, the compulsions are conditioned responses to anxiety. This anxiety is brought on by obsessive thoughts about contamination, doubt, fear of self-harm, and the like. The performance of a compulsive behavior, such as hand washing, is the conditioned response that temporarily reduces the stress brought on by the obsessive thought. However, by performing the compulsive behavior, the subject never actually receives a chance to habituate to the anxiety caused by the obsessional thought, but only transiently avoids feeling more anxious. Thus, this compulsion actually reinforces the obsession (Rachman and Hodgson 1980). For OCD symptoms to be treated, the patient must habituate to the anxiety provoked by his or her obsessions instead of performing compulsions. As anxiety decreases and compulsions are prevented, the urge to ritualize declines. The type of treatment employing this model is called ERP and is elaborated in the "Treatment" section below.

Psychodynamic Theory

The contributions of psychodynamic theory have been in the understanding of the etiology of OCD more from a psychodynamic than a neurobiological formulation. Although such psychodynamic understanding alone rarely contributes to significant reduction in symptoms, it can play a role in the overall understanding and treatment of the patient, especially in cases where prominent or excessive doubt, poor insight, and fear of losing control, all features of treatment resistance, are part of the clinical picture.

Freud's model for understanding OCD postulates that obsessions and compulsions develop through fixation on or regression to the anal-sadistic stage of development. Prominent features of this stage of development are issues relating to control, aggression, and autonomy. Management of impulses and conflicts that develop at this stage is accomplished through the defense mechanisms of reaction formation, isolation, and undoing. The repetitive rituals and compulsions seen in OCD patients exemplify this doing and undoing behavior. In addition, issues around control often contribute to patients' willingness to take medications or change compulsive behaviors.

Treatment

General Considerations

Before the 1980s, it was believed that OCD was a rare and treatment-resistant disorder. However, the epidemiological and treatment data collected since the 1980s have changed this clinical picture, so that most clinicians view OCD as a common disorder with approximately a 2%–3% prevalence (Karno et al. 1988; Robins et al. 1984) in which the majority of patients (60%–80%) exhibit some response to treatment—pharmacological, behavioral, or both (Jenike 1992). However, the key features of OCD, as already discussed, include obsessional doubt, a need to feel in control, and risk aversion, and these features have a significant bearing on the successful application of both pharmacological and behavioral treatments.

Obsessional doubt and risk aversion are often initial barriers to treatment. The clinician may often find him- or herself with a patient who doubts that treatment will be successful and who is unwilling to deal with the risk of side effects or the anxiety that behavioral treatment will evoke. Often, the clinician must take extra time to explain the benefits of treatment that make it worth the risk.

In addition, the OCD patient's cognitive misperceptions often lead to beliefs that he or she will experience each and every side effect to the most severe degree or that the anxiety evoked by the ERP will be totally unbearable. This cognitive distortion leads the patient to see everything in extremes. Again, the clinician must take extra time to inform without provoking irrational concerns, thus providing a corrective cognitive experience. Giving accurate data on side effects also includes correcting cognitive distortions. In this regard, it is important to identify for patients that their OCD and fear of risk may be contributing to their trepidation about medications and that although there are many side effects, especially with clomipramine, they will not get every one, or even experience the side effects at an intensity that is unbearable. In the case of fear about overwhelming anxiety from behavioral interventions, it can be helpful to have patients actually write down their worst fears in a scripted imagery and read them over and over. Often, simply writing them down helps patients to see the irrational nature of their fears, and by reading the script over and over, they can begin to habituate to the anxiety.

Fear of losing control can also manifest itself throughout treatment. In the case of behavioral treatment, patients may feel, based on the anxiety provoked, that they are moving too quickly. However, by setting up their own hierarchy of behaviors, patients can feel in control of the pace and rate at which they move forward. Because treatment response to pharmacological agents for OCD usually requires 6–10 weeks, patients have plenty of time to get accustomed to the medicine, and, therefore, the issue of control of the pace during medication trials is less prominent. However, the issue of control often arises in the long duration of treatment required before any treatment effect is usually seen. Issues around doubt can enter the treatment as the patient becomes frustrated by an absence of symptom improvement in the face of significant side effects. For this reason, preparing the patient in the early stages of treatment for what to anticipate over the course of treatment is very helpful in maintaining treatment compliance.

When insight is poor, as in more delusional OCD, or severe anxiety is a comorbid symptom, the patient may be unable or unwilling to engage in behavioral treatment. In such cases, it may be better to start with medication and achieve some initial reduction in symptoms or improvement in insight before engaging in behavioral treatment.

Assessment

The most widely used measure in treatment outcome studies is the Y-BOCS. This scale was developed on the basis of clinical interviews with OCD subjects in the 1980s. Unlike instruments that preceded it, the Y-BOCS measures severity rather than types of symptoms, and its 10 questions can be divided into two parallel subscales, one for obsessions and one for compulsions, each with a potential score of 20, adding up to an overall total score of 40. In general, patients scoring at least 16–18 are considered ill enough to require treatment, and those scoring over 30 are considered severely ill (Pato et al. 1994). In terms of treatment outcome, a 25%–35% reduction is felt to represent significant improvement in symptoms (Goodman et al. 1993). It can be helpful to use the Y-BOCS in everyday clinical practice as well as in the research setting as a measure of symptom improvement and, as such, a justification for remaining on a given medication or switching to another. The key to obtaining a valid measure of symptom severity with the Y-BOCS is eliciting a careful history of the patient's specific symptoms, both obsessions and compulsions. This can be done with the help of the Y-BOCS symptom checklist. The patient version of this checklist can actually be given to the patient to complete; it contains a list of symptoms with easy-to-understand explanations of what each symptom is.

Pharmacological Treatments

As previously discussed in the section on etiology and pathophysiology, the serotonin system and, more specifically, serotonin reuptake inhibitors have been found to be an integral part of the pharmacological treatment of OCD. These agents include clomipramine, fluoxetine, sertraline, paroxetine, and fluvoxamine. All are currently available in the United States, and all have OCD among their indications. Clomipramine (Anafranil) was the first agent to receive U.S. Food and Drug Administration (FDA) approval for the treatment of OCD and thus was the first to have large multicenter placebo-controlled data available (Clomipramine Collaborative Study Group 1991). Other agents have followed with similar placebo-controlled multicenter studies: fluoxetine (Prozac; Tollefson et al. 1994a, 1994b; Wood et al. 1993), sertraline (Zoloft; Greist et al. 1995c), paroxetine (Paxil; Wheadon et al. 1993), and fluvoxamine (Luvox; Greist et al. 1995a; Rasmussen et al., in press). Ideally, the choice of a pharmacological agent for treating OCD would be based on comparative efficacy of the different serotonin reuptake–inhibiting agents available. However, the choice of treatment is difficult for two major reasons: 1) lack of large comparative efficacy trials (although some small trials have studied clomipramine versus fluoxetine [Pigott et al. 1990] and clomipramine versus fluvoxamine [Freeman et al. 1994; Koran et al. 1996]), and 2) differences in side-effect profiles.

Despite the lack of head-to-head comparison data, comparative efficacies have been gleaned from meta-analyses of these large, controlled studies on individual drugs (Greist et al. 1995b; Jenike et al. 1990a). However, such analyses are not without their problems. These include differences in dosing strategies, differences in illness severity of those treated, and heterogeneity of subject pools. The latter issue reflects the 10-year time course over which these clinical trials have been conducted. In the beginning of this decade, during which clomipramine was tested, most patients who sought treatment had never been treated for their OCD. In the later portion of the period, during which trials of sertraline, paroxetine, and fluvoxamine were conducted, many of the subjects entering the studies had already received trials of clomipramine or fluoxetine, which were readily available. Several authors have attributed the smaller effect sizes of newer agents, as well as the larger placebo response rates seen with these agents, to this factor (Greist et al. 1995b; Jenike et al. 1990b).

Given these limitations, the following conclusions can be drawn. The overall effect size seen with clomipramine has been consistently higher than that with the SSRIs, although fluoxetine, sertraline, fluvoxamine, and paroxetine all have shown good efficacy compared with placebo in the treatment of OCD (Freeman et al. 1994; Jefferson and Greist 1996; Koran et al. 1996; Pigott 1996). Comparative tolerability has been a mixed picture. In terms of side effects (see Table 12–1), clomipramine clearly has more than any of the SSRIs. A number of studies have reported that a greater number of patients experience some side effects with clomipramine (between 80% and 97%) than with either fluoxetine or paroxetine (Greist et al. 1995c; Jenike et al. 1990a; Pigott et al. 1990; Tollefson et al. 1994b; Wheadon et al. 1993; Wood et al. 1993), whereas others have shown similarly high side-effect frequencies with other SSRIs, including sertraline and fluvoxamine (Freeman et al. 1994; Greist et al. 1995b; Koran et al. 1996). However, such findings must be viewed with caution, since it is not always easy to measure the severity—or rather, the significance—of side effects. For instance, is "very dry mouth" as big a problem as "mild impotency"? Such a judgment would depend on the patient's interpretation of the symptoms. Thus, many clinicians and researchers have turned to comparative dropout rates rather than number or intensity of side effects to provide an indirect measure of the tolerability of a medication. The results in this regard have been mixed but interesting. In comparative studies of fluvoxamine and clomipramine (Freeman et al. 1994; Koran et al. 1996), dropout rates were virtually identical for both medications, around 15%. However, in a meta-analysis, Greist et al. (1995c) noted that analysis of the pooled multicenter studies revealed the lowest rates of dropout in the clomipramine group (12%), followed by fluoxetine (23%), fluvoxamine (24%), and sertraline (27%).

Another important consideration in treatment is cross-responsivity. *Cross-responsivity* refers to the probability of a patient's responding to a second antiobsessional agent if he or she has already responded to one antiobsessional agent—or, on a more pessimistic note, whether a patient will respond to a second or third agent if he or she has failed to respond to previous agents. Although data are sparse in this regard, those available are hopeful. In a multicenter trial of fluvoxamine (Rasmussen et al., in press), 19% of patients who had failed to respond to previous trials with clomipramine or fluoxetine responded to fluvoxamine. In an analysis of a small trial comparing fluoxetine and clomipramine, Pigott (1996) noted that only 65% of patients who responded to clomipramine also responded to fluoxetine, whereas 80% of patients who responded to fluoxetine also responded to clomipramine. On the negative side, patients who had not responded to clomipramine had only a 20% chance of responding to fluoxetine. Thus, it would appear that if an initial agent is unsuccessful, it is reasonable to pursue a trial with other agents, and that response to clomipramine is the best harbinger of responsivity to other agents.

Duration of Treatment

Clinical recommendations for duration of treatment differ significantly from the 2–4 weeks recommended for depression. Numerous trials with various antiobsessional agents have demonstrated that most patients do not begin to respond until 4–6 weeks of treatment and that a full 10-week trial at an adequate dose (see "Dosing," below) is needed before a trial can be deemed sufficient (Goodman et al. 1989a; Greist et al. 1995a, 1995b; Jefferson and Greist 1996; Jenike et al. 1990a; Ras-

Table 12–1. Common side effects of serotonergic medications (occurring in more than 10% of individuals)

Clomipramine[a,b]	Fluoxetine[c]	Fluvoxamine[a,d]	Sertraline[e]	Paroxetine[f]
abnormal vision	decreased libido	asthenia	anorexia	asthenia
anorexia	dry mouth	dyspepsia[a]	decreased libido	decreased appetite
constipation[a]	nausea	headache[a]	diarrhea	dry mouth
dizziness	somnolence	insomnia[a]	headache	insomnia
dry mouth[a]		nausea	insomnia	nausea
fatigue		nervousness[a]	nausea	sexual dysfunction
insomnia		somnolence		somnolence
micturition disorder				tremor
myoclonus				
nausea				
nervousness				
postural hypotension[a]				
sexual dysfunction				
somnolence				
sweating				
tremor				

[a] Koran 1996; Freeman 1994 (clomipramine vs. fluvoxamine); Koran found that dry mouth, constipation, and postural hypotension were more common with clomipramine, whereas insomnia, nervousness, dyspepsia, and headache were more common with fluvoxamine.
[b] Clomipramine Collaborative Study Group 1991 (clomipramine vs. placebo).
[c] Tollefson 1994 (fluoxetine vs. placebo).
[d] Greist 1995a (fluvoxamine vs. placebo).
[e] Greist 1995b (sertraline vs. placebo).
[f] Wheadon 1993 (paroxetine vs. placebo).

mussen et al. 1993; Rasmussen et al., in press). This long treatment trial can raise some significant issues in terms of compliance, as already noted. However, given that the typical patient with OCD has experienced symptoms for many years, most are willing to endure this long treatment trial if its necessity is explained.

Dosing

The issue of how much medication to give a patient has recently received more systematic study. Clinical wisdom still maintains that maximal doses of each of the antiobsessional agents be given. For clomipramine, the maximum dose is 250 mg/day; doses higher than this significantly increase the risk of seizures (DeVeaugh-Geiss et al. 1989). For fluoxetine, the maximum dose is 80 mg/day, although fluoxetine's exceptionally long half-life may complicate washout (DeVane 1994; Pato et al. 1991). For sertraline, the maximum dose is 200 mg/day, and for fluvoxamine and paroxetine, 300 mg/day and 60 mg/day, respectively. A trial of 10–12 weeks should still be pursued with any one of these medications before abandoning its use.

The results of recent fixed-dose studies of three agents—fluoxetine (Tollefson et al. 1994a, 1994b; Wood et al. 1993), sertraline (Greist et al. 1995a), and paroxetine (Wheadon et al. 1993)—should cause clinicians to reconsider the steps in dosing for initial treatment, keeping in mind that fixed-dose studies of clomipramine and fluvoxamine have not yet been reported. The fluoxetine fixed-dose studies are noteworthy because they showed effectiveness at all three doses studied—20, 40, and 60 mg (Tollefson et al. 1994a, 1994b; Wood et al. 1993). However, there was a trend toward 60 mg being more effective, and in a follow-up study in which patients were allowed to increase their dose from that used in the initial trial, patients demonstrated increased improvement at higher doses. Furthermore, this improvement was either maintained or increased further over the 5–6 months of follow-up (Levine et al. 1989; Tollefson et al. 1994a). In the paroxetine fixed-dose study (Wheadon et al. 1993), patients did not respond to the lower dose of 20 mg but needed higher doses of 40 or 60 mg to show improvement in their obsessive-compulsive symptoms. Perhaps the most interesting, if problematic, data have come from the sertraline trials (Greist et al. 1995b). In this study, 50 mg and 200 mg showed therapeutic benefit in all four measures of improvement (Y-BOCS, National Institute of Mental Health Global Obsessive-Compulsive [NIMH-GOC], and Clinical Global Impression [CGI] Severity and Improvement) but the 100-mg dose showed improvement only in one global measure (NIMH-GOC). Such results are not easy to explain, except perhaps by noting that patients who do not respond at 50 mg may need to be tried at 200 mg before they are considered nonresponders to sertraline.

Jefferson and Greist (1996) note that although these different doses are effective, higher doses are associated with more frequent and more severe side effects. Thus, it seems advisable to ask patients to tolerate the wait of using a lower dose of medication for 10 weeks before trying a higher one. Clinically, a compromise might be struck by the clinician. Whereas most researchers recommend 10 weeks for an adequate trial, many have noted some response beginning at 4 weeks (Greist et al. 1995b, 1995c). Thus, the clinician could start a patient at a low dose and then switch him or her to a higher dose in 4–6 weeks if no response is seen at the lesser dose. Although such a strategy might miss some "late responders" (Rasmussen et al., in press) to the lower dose, it could reduce the overall duration of a treatment trial of two different doses from 20 weeks to 14 weeks.

It is worth noting that the SSRIs, via their effect on the cytochrome P450 system, can inhibit the metabolism of certain other drugs. This effect is best documented for fluoxetine, which has been shown to elevate blood levels of a variety of coadministered drugs, including various tricyclics (e.g., clomipramine), carbamazepine, phenytoin, and trazodone (DeVane 1994). However, other SSRIs may cause similar elevations. Thus, the clinician may have to base the choice of medication on what the patient is already taking or adjust the dose of other medications when these SSRIs are used.

Recommendations

Taking into consideration comparative efficacy and comparative tolerability data, general recommendations for pharmacological treatment are that an adequate pharmacological trial must consider the use of multiple agents, including clomipramine. High doses (up to the manufacturer's recommended maximums) should be used if lower doses are not effective. Finally, whereas some benefit may be seen as early as 4 weeks, an adequate duration of pharmacological treatment for OCD is considered to be 10–12 weeks at maximum tolerated doses (Rasmussen et al. 1993). Although it is reassuring to know that continued medication administration will afford many patients continued improvement, patients often wish to stop medication for a variety of reasons, including cost, a desire to become pregnant, or unwanted side effects such as weight gain or sexual dysfunction. The only double-blind, controlled discontinuation trials have involved clomipramine. There have been three such studies, one with adults (Pato et al. 1988) and two with children (Leonard et al. 1989, 1991). All three of these reports, as well as anecdotal ones, have shown that approximately 90% of patients experience a return of symptoms within 4 to 7 weeks of discontinuing treatment or, in the case of the child studies, of substituting desipramine for clomipramine.

As noted by Jefferson and Greist (1996), these recommendations for medication regimens are based on clinical research. How a medication performs in the clinical arena of private practice is often quite different from how it performs in a carefully controlled research study. For this reason, some helpful clinical algorithms have been developed (Jefferson and Greist 1996; see Figure 12–1) to provide a flexible framework for the clinician in treating OCD patients.

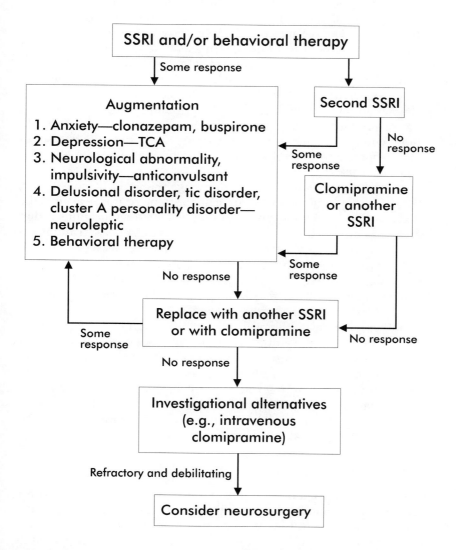

Figure 12–1. Algorithm of OCD treatment. OCD = obsessive-compulsive disorder; SSRI = selective serotonin reuptake inhibitor; TCA = tricyclic antidepressant.

Resistance to Treatment and Augmentation Strategies

Some data provide information about the characteristics of patients who are more resistant to treatment. In particular, patients with schizotypal personality disorder, borderline personality disorder, avoidant personality disorder, and obsessive-compulsive personality disorder have shown poorer response to pharmacotherapy in some studies. Thus, accurate diagnosis is a crucial aspect of assessing treatment resistance. However, perhaps more importantly, before giving a patient the label of treatment-resistant, one needs to assess the adequacy of each medication trial from the point of both dose (was it high enough?) and duration (was it long enough?). In addition, given the data on cross-responsivity, one should note which medications have been tried and whether one of them has been clomipramine. Finally, if adequate doses of primary medications have been given, the clinician should explore whether augmenting agents were given, especially in cases of partial response to monotherapy (Goodman et al. 1993; Jenike 1993; Jenike et al. 1986).

Although the use of an augmenting agent should be considered, clinical wisdom suggests that if there has been no response at all to the initial agent, it is probably better to simply switch medications rather than add an augmenting agent (Jefferson and Greist 1996). If augmenting agents are used, a trial of 2 weeks or, in some cases (e.g., buspirone), up to 8 weeks may be warranted (Goodman et al. 1993; Jenike 1993; Jenike et al. 1991). Overall, most augmenting agents have not performed well in systematic trials, although a number of anecdotal reports have shown them to be effective in some patients.

Another potential guideline for choosing an augmenting agent is the presence of comorbid symptoms in the patient. For instance, if poor insight or psychosis is present, one might add an antipsychotic such as pimozide (McDougle et al. 1990) or risperidone (Jacobsen 1995). With prominent anxiety features, one might consider buspirone (Jenike et al. 1991; Markovitz et al. 1990; McDougle et al. 1993; Pigott et al. 1992a), trazodone (Pigott et al. 1992b), or clonazepam, and, with mood lability, lithium (McDougle et al. 1991).

Psychosurgery

In recent years, psychosurgical techniques have been examined for their potential benefit in extremely severe cases of OCD that have been unresponsive to two to three adequate medication trials with augmentation and to adequate trials of behavioral therapy. Small studies with very well-defined samples have showed success rates of 55%–67% without significant side effects (Mindus and Jenike 1992). Techniques have included surgical procedures such as anterior capsulotomy, cingulotomy, and limbic leukotomy. Noninvasive surgical techniques such as gamma knife procedures are also being explored.

Behavioral Therapy

Behavioral therapy—specifically, ERP—has been successfully used for the treatment of OCD since the late 1970s (Foa et al. 1985; Greist 1994; Marks et al. 1980, 1988). Recent studies that used PET scans before and after behavioral and pharmacological treatment (Baxter et al. 1992; Schwartz et al. 1996) have further reinforced these positive assessments of the efficacy of behavioral therapy. These studies have shown that pharmacotherapy and behavioral therapy produce similar decreases in brain activity. In addition, the areas of the brain that are affected by behavioral treatment have, in many cases, also been identified as areas of brain abnormality from other imaging techniques (Breiter et al. 1996; Rauch et al. 1994; Swedo et al. 1992).

The basic principles underlying ERP are that compulsions provide only a temporary reduction of the anxiety produced by obsessions. Furthermore, the only way to experience more permanent relief is to habituate to the anxiety caused by the obsession without performing the compulsion. Habituation is the key factor, and clinicians proceed by first identifying triggers and situations that bring on obsessional thoughts and compulsive behaviors and then developing a graduated hierarchy of anxiety based on the patient's report. The patient "challenges" him- or herself with the least anxiety-provoking items first and then moves up the hierarchy. In addition to exposure, the patient is instructed to refrain from carrying out the associated rituals. These techniques have shown particular success with washing rituals (Jenike 1993) but can be adapted to almost any type of compulsions, including mental rituals, with some creativity. For instance, traditional wisdom held that mental rituals were difficult to treat because the lack of observable behavior (compulsions) created an obstacle to response prevention. However, effective ERP has been accomplished with scripted imagery and continuous-loop tapes in which patients record their obsessional fears and mental compulsions and then expose themselves to these materials over and over again until they have habituated. Another recent innovation in behavioral treatment is treatment in a group setting with and without family members (Fals-Stewart et al. 1993; Livingston–Van Noppen et al. 1991). Not only is group treatment equally effective and more cost efficient than individual treatment, but the group cohesion lends mutual support and encouragement to the participants in behavioral treatment. In addition, as Calvocoressi et al. (1995) and others have demonstrated, families are often directly or indirectly affected by the patient's OCD, so including family members in treatment is often critical to optimizing recovery.

An added benefit of behavioral treatment is its long-term efficacy. Unlike pharmacotherapy, whose palliative effects do not persist in the great majority of patients after medication is discontinued (Pato et al. 1988), behavioral therapy has shown continued efficacy in follow-up studies ranging from 1 to 6 years, although booster sessions may be needed (O'Sullivan and Marks 1991).

Yet despite its benefits, behavioral treatment is not for everyone. About 15%–25% of patients refuse, at least initially, to engage in behavioral therapy because of its anxiety-provoking nature (Greist 1994), and another 25% fail to benefit from treatment (Foa et al. 1983; Greist 1994), leaving only about 50%–70% of patients initially responsive to this treatment. These statistics may improve, however, in a comprehensive program that includes behavioral, pharmacological, and other support networks for patients and family members. Integrated programs encourage patients, over time, to stay in treatment and to pursue modalities that they initially were unwilling to consider or unsuccessful in sustaining.

Conclusions

OCD is a prevalent illness in adulthood that often presents comorbidly with other disorders. Increasingly, it appears to have a strong biological and genetic basis. OCD is quite responsive to treatment, especially combined treatment with medications that have some impact on the serotonin system and behavioral therapy that specifically includes ERP. These modalities produce symptom improvement in up to 85% of patients. However, unlike the case for other illnesses such as depressive and anxiety disorders, few OCD patients achieve total remission (i.e., "cure") of their symptoms. Yet for most patients, even a modest improvement of 15%–25% can make a significant difference in their overall functioning.

References

American Psychiatric Association: Diagnostic and Statistical Manual of Mental Disorders, 3rd Edition. Washington, DC, American Psychiatric Association, 1984

American Psychiatric Association: Diagnostic and Statistical Manual of Mental Disorders, 3rd Edition, Revised. Washington, DC, American Psychiatric Association, 1987

American Psychiatric Association: Diagnostic and Statistical Manual of Mental Disorders, 4th Edition. Washington, DC, American Psychiatric Association, 1994

Baer L, Jenike MA, Ricciardi JN, et al: Standardized assessment of personality disorders in obsessive-compulsive disorder. Arch Gen Psychiatry 47:826–830, 1990

Barr LL, Goodman WK, McDougle LJ, et al: Tryptophan depletion in patients with obsessive-compulsive disorder who respond to serotonin reuptake inhibitors. Arch Gen Psychiatry 51:309–317, 1994

Baxter LR, Schwartz JM, Mazziotta JC, et al: Cerebral glucose metabolic rates in nonde-pressed patients with obsessive-compulsive disorder. Am J Psychiatry 145:1560–1563, 1988

Baxter LR, Schwartz JM, Bergman KS, et al: Caudate glucose metabolic rate changes with both drug and behavior therapy for obsessive-compulsive disorder. Arch Gen Psychiatry 49:681–689, 1992

Bellodi L, Sciuto G, Diaferia G, et al: Psychiatric disorders in the families of patients with obsessive-compulsive disorder. Psychiatry Res 42:111–120, 1992

Benkelfat C, Nordahl TE, Semple WE, et al: Local cerebral glucose metabolic rates in ob-sessive-compulsive disorder: patients treated with clomipramine. Arch Gen Psychia-try 47:840–848, 1990

Black DW, Noyes R, Goldstein RB, et al: A family study of obsessive compulsive disorder. Arch Gen Psychiatry 49:362–368, 1992

Breiter HC, Rauch SL, Kwong KK, et al: Functional magnetic resonance imaging of symp-tom provocation in obsessive compulsive disorder. Arch Gen Psychiatry 53:595–606, 1996

Calvocoressi LC, Lewis B, Harris M, et al: Family accommodation in obsessive-compul-sive disorder. Am J Psychiatry 152:441–443, 1995

Clomipramine Collaborative Study Group: Efficacy of clomipramine in OCD: results of a multicenter double-blind trial. Arch Gen Psychiatry 48:730–738, 1991

DeVane CL: Pharmacokinetics of the selective serotonin reuptake inhibitors. J Clin Psy-chiatry 53 (2, suppl):13–20, 1992

DeVane CL: Pharmacogenetics and drug metabolism of newer antidepressant agents. J Clin Psychiatry 55 (12, suppl):38–45, 1994

DeVeaugh-Geiss J, Landau P, Katz R: Treatment of obsessive-compulsive disorder with clomipramine. Psychiatric Annals 19:97–101, 1989

Eisen JL, Rasmussen SA: Obsessive-compulsive disorder with psychotic features. J Clin Psychiatry 54:373–379, 1993

Fals-Stewart W, Marks AP, Schafer J: A comparison of behavioral group therapy and indi-vidual behavioral therapy in treating obsessive compulsive disorder. J Nerv Ment Dis 18:189–193, 1993

Flament MF, Rapoport JL, Murphy DL, et al: Biochemical changes during clomipramine treatment of childhood obsessive-compulsive disorder. Arch Gen Psychiatry 44:219–225, 1987

Foa EB: Failure in treating obsessive-compulsives. Behav Res Ther 17:169–176, 1979

Foa EB, Kozak MJ: DSM-IV field trial: obsessive-compulsive disorder. Am J Psychiatry 152:90–96, 1995

Foa EB, Grayson JB, Steketee GS, et al: Success and failure in the behavioral treatment of obsessive-compulsives. J Consult Clin Psychol 51:287–297, 1983

Foa EB, Steketee GS, Ozarow BJ: Behavior therapy with obsessive-compulsives: from the-ory to treatment, in Obsessive-Compulsive Disorder: Psychological and Pharmaco-logical Treatment. Edited by Mavissakalian M, Turner SM, Michelson L. New York, Plenum, 1985, pp 49–129

Freeman CPL, Trimble MR, Deakin JFW, et al: Fluvoxamine versus clomipramine in the treatment of obsessive-compulsive disorder: a multicenter randomized, double-blind, parallel group comparison. J Clin Psychiatry 55:301–305, 1994

Goodman WK, Price LH, Rasmussen SA, et al: Efficacy of fluvoxamine in obsessive com-pulsive disorder: a double-blind comparison with placebo. Arch Gen Psychiatry 46:36–44, 1989a

Goodman WK, Price LH, Rasmussen SA, et al: The Yale-Brown Obsessive Compulsive Scale, I: development, use, and reliability. Arch Gen Psychiatry 46:1006–1011, 1989b

Goodman WK, McDougle CJ, Lawrence HP, et al: Beyond the serotonin hypothesis: a role for dopamine in some forms of obsessive-compulsive disorder. J Clin Psychopharma-col 51 (8, suppl):36–43, 1990

Goodman WK, McDougle CJ, Barr LC, et al: Biological approaches to treatment-resistant obsessive-compulsive disorder. J Clin Psychiatry 54 (6, suppl):16–26, 1993

Greist JH: Behavior therapy for obsessive compulsive disorder. J Clin Psychiatry 55 (10, suppl):60–68, 1994

Greist JH, Charnard G, Duboff E, et al: Double-blind parallel comparison of three dosages of sertraline and placebo in outpatients with obsessive-compulsive disorder. Arch Gen Psychiatry 52:53–60, 1995a

Greist JH, Jefferson JW, Kobak KA, et al: Efficacy and tolerability of serotonin transport inhibitors in obsessive-compulsive disorder. Arch Gen Psychiatry 52:53–60, 1995b

Greist JH, Jenike MA, Robinson D, et al: Efficacy of fluvoxamine in obsessive compulsive disorder: results of a multicentre, double-blind placebo-controlled trial. European Journal of Clinical Research __:195–204, 1995c

Hewlett WA, Martin K: Fenfluramine challenges and serotonergic functioning in obsessive compulsive disorder. Paper presented at the First International Obsessive-Compulsive Disorder Congress, Capri, Italy, March 12–13, 1993

Hoehn-Saric R, Pearlson G, Harris G, et al: Effects of fluoxetine on regional cerebral blood flow in obsessive-compulsive patients. Am J Psychiatry 148:1243–1245, 1991

Hollander E: Introduction, in Obsessive-Compulsive Related Disorders. Edited by Hollander E. Washington, DC, American Psychiatric Press, 1993, pp 1–16

Hollander E, DeCaria C, Nitescu A, et al: Serotonergic function in obsessive-compulsive disorder: behavioral and neuroendocrine responses to oral m-chlorophenylpiperazine and fenfluramine in patients and healthy volunteers. Arch Gen Psychiatry 49:21–28, 1992

Insel TR: Toward a neuroanatomy of obsessive-compulsive disorder. Arch Gen Psychiatry 49:739–744, 1992

Insel TR, Akiskal HS: Obsessive-compulsive disorder with psychotic features: a phenomenological analysis. Am J Psychiatry 143:1527–1533, 1986

Insel TR, Winslow JT: Neurobiology of obsessive-compulsive disorder. Psychiatr Clin North Am 15:813–824, 1992

Insel T, Murphy D, Cohen R, et al: Obsessive-compulsive disorder: a double-blind study of clomipramine and clorgyline. Arch Gen Psychiatry 40:605–612, 1983

Jacobsen FM: Risperidone in the treatment of affective illness and obsessive-compulsive disorder. J Clin Psychiatry 56:423–429, 1995

Jefferson JQ, Greist JH: The pharmacotherapy of obsessive-compulsive disorder. Psychiatric Annals 26:202–209, 1996

Jenike MA: Pharmacologic treatment of obsessive-compulsive disorders. Psychiatr Clin North Am 15:895–919, 1992

Jenike MA: Augmentation strategies for treatment-resistant obsessive compulsive disorder. Harvard Review of Psychiatry 1:17–26, 1993

Jenike MA, Baer L, Minichiello WE, et al: Concomitant obsessive-compulsive disorder and schizotypal personality disorder. Am J Psychiatry 143:530–532, 1986

Jenike MA, Baer L, Greist JH: Clomipramine versus fluoxetine in obsessive-compulsive disorder: a retrospective comparison of side effects and efficacy. J Clin Psychopharmacol 10:122–124, 1990a

Jenike MA, Hyman SE, Baer L, et al: A controlled trial of fluvoxamine for obsessive-compulsive disorder: implications for a serotonergic theory. Am J Psychiatry 147:1209–1215, 1990b

Jenike MA, Baer L, Buttolph L: Buspirone augmentation of fluoxetine in patients with obsessive compulsive disorder. J Clin Psychiatry 1:13–14, 1991

Karno M, Golding JM, Sorenson SB, et al: The epidemiology of obsessive compulsive disorder in five U.S. communities. Arch Gen Psychiatry 45:1094–1099, 1988

Koran LM, McElroy SL, Davidson JRT, et al: Fluvoxamine vs clomipramine for obsessive-compulsive disorder: a double-blind comparison. J Clin Psychopharmacol 16:121–129, 1996

Kozak MJ, Foa EB: Obsessions, overvalued ideas, and delusions in obsessive-compulsive disorder. Behavior Res Ther 32:343–353, 1994

Lees AJ, Robertson M, Trimble MR, et al: A clinical study of Gilles de la Tourette syndrome in the United Kingdom. J Neurol Neurosurg Psychiatry 47:1–8, 1984

Lelliott PT, Noshirvani HF, Basoglu M, et al: Obsessive-compulsive beliefs and treatment outcome. Psychol Med 18:697–702, 1988

Lenane MC, Swedo SE, Leonard H, et al: Psychiatric disorders in first-degree relatives of children and adolescents with obsessive compulsive disorder. J Am Acad Child Adolesc Psychiatry 29:407–412, 1990

Leonard HL, Swedo SE, Rapport JL, et al: Treatment of childhood obsessive-compulsive disorders with clomipramine and desipramine: a double-blind crossover comparison. Arch Gen Psychiatry 46:1088–1092, 1989

Leonard HL, Swedo SE, Lenane MD, et al: A double-blind desipramine substitution during long-term clomipramine treatment in children and adolescents with obsessive compulsive disorder. Arch Gen Psychiatry 922–927, 1991

Leonard HL, Lenane MC, Swedo SE, et al: Tics and Tourette's disorder: a 2- to 7-year follow-up of 54 obsessive-compulsive children. Am J Psychiatry 149:1244–1251, 1992

Levine R, Hoffman JS, Knepple ED, et al: Long-term fluoxetine treatment of a large number of obsessive compulsive patients. J Clin Psychopharmacol 9:281–283, 1989

Livingston–Van Noppen B, Rasmussen SA, McCartney L, et al: A multi-family group approach as an adjunct to treatment of obsessive compulsive disorders, in Current Treatments of Obsessive-Compulsive Disorder. Edited by Pato MT, Zohar J. Washington, DC, American Psychiatric Press, 1991, pp 115–134

Mavissakalian M, Jones B, Olson S, et al: Clomipramine in obsessive-compulsive disorder: clinical response and plasma levels. J Clin Psychopharmacology 10:261–268, 1990

Markovitz PJ, Stagnos J, Calabresa JR: Buspirone augmentation of fluoxetine on obsessive compulsive disorder. Am J Psychiatry 147:798–800, 1990

Marks I, Stern A, Mawson D, et al: Clomipramine and exposure for obsessive-compulsive rituals. Br J Psychiatry 136:1–25, 1980

Marks I, Lelliott P, Basoglu M, et al: Clomipramine, self-exposure and therapist-added exposure in obsessive-compulsive ritualizers. Br J Psychiatry 152:522–534, 1988

McDougle CJ, Goodman WK, Price LH, et al: Neuroleptic addition in fluvoxamine refractory obsessive compulsive disorder. Am J Psychiatry 147:652–654, 1990

McDougle CJ, Price LH, Goodman WK, et al: A controlled trial of lithium augmentation in fluvoxamine refractory obsessive compulsive disorder: lack of efficacy. J Clin Psychopharmacol 11:175–184, 1991

McDougle CJ, Goodman WK, Leckman JF, et al: Limited therapeutic effect of addition of buspirone in fluvoxamine refractory obsessive compulsive disorder. Am J Psychiatry 150:647–649, 1993

McKeon P, Murray R: Familial aspects of obsessive compulsive neurosis. Br J Psychiatry 51:528–534, 1987

Mindus P, Jenike MA: Neurosurgical treatment of malignant obsessive compulsive disorder. Psychiatr Clin North Am 15:921–938, 1992

Montgomery SA: Pharmacological treatment of obsessive-compulsive disorder, in Current Insights in Obsessive-Compulsive Disorder. Edited by Hollander E, Zohar J, Marazziti D, et al. West Sussex, UK, John Wiley & Sons, 1994, pp 214–225

Nordahl TE, Benkelfat C, Semple WE, et al: Cerebral glucose metabolic rates in obsessive compulsive disorder. Neuropsychopharmacology 2:23–28, 1989

O'Sullivan G, Marks I: Follow-up studies of behavioral treatment of phobia and obsessive compulsive neurosis. Psychiatric Annals 21:368–373, 1991

Pato MT, Zohar-Kadouch R, Zohar J, et al: Return of symptoms after discontinuation of clomipramine in patients with obsessive compulsive disorder. Am J Psychiatry 145:1521–1525, 1988

Pato MT, Murphy DL, DeVane CL: Sustained plasma concentrations of fluoxetine and/or norfluoxetine 4 and 8 weeks after fluoxetine discontinuation. J Clin Psychopharmacol 11:224–225, 1991

Pato MT, Eisen JL, Pato CN: Rating scales for obsessive-compulsive disorder, in Current Insights in Obsessive-Compulsive Disorder. Edited by Hollander E, Zohar J, Marazziti D, et al. West Sussex, UK, John Wiley & Sons, 1994, pp 77–92

Pauls DL, Towbin KE, Leckman JF, et al: Gilles de la Tourette's syndrome and obsessive-compulsive disorder: evidence supporting a genetic relationship. Arch Gen Psychiatry 43:1180–1182, 1986

Pauls DL, Raymond CL, Stevenson JF, et al: A family study of Gilles de la Tourette's syndrome. Am J Hum Genet 48:154–163, 1991

Pauls DL, Alsobrook MP, Goodman W, et al: A family study of obsessive compulsive disorder. Am J Psychiatry 152:76–84, 1995

Phillips KA: Body dysmorphic disorder: the distress of imagined ugliness. Am J Psychiatry 148:1138–1149, 1991

Phillips KA, McElroy SL, Hudson JI, et al: Body dysmorphic disorder: an OCD spectrum disorder, a form of affective spectrum disorder, or both? J Clin Psychiatry 56 (4, suppl):41–51, 1995

Pigott TA: OCD: where the serotonin selective story begins. J Clin Psychiatry 57 (6, suppl):11–20, 1996

Pigott TA, Pato MT, Bernstein SE, et al: Controlled comparison of clomipramine and fluoxetine in the treatment of obsessive-compulsive disorder. Arch Gen Psychiatry 47:926–932, 1990

Pigott TA, Zohar J, Hill JL, et al: Metergoline blocks the behavioral and neuroendocrine effects of orally administered *m*-chlorophenylpiperazine in patients with obsessive-compulsive disorder. Biol Psychiatry 29:418–426, 1991

Pigott TA, L'Hereux F, Hill JL, et al: A double-blind study of adjuvant buspirone hydrochloride in clomipramine-treated patients with obsessive compulsive disorder. J Clin Psychopharmacol 12:11–18, 1992a

Pigott TA, Littenfer XF, Rubenstein CS, et al: A double-blind, placebo-controlled study of trazodone in patients with obsessive compulsive disorder. J Clin Psychopharmacol 12:156–162, 1992b

Pitman RK: Historical considerations, in Psychobiology of Obsessive Compulsive Disorder. Edited by Zohar J, Insel T, Rasmussen S. New York, Springer-Verlag, 1991, pp 1–12

Rachman SJ, Hodgson RJ: Obsessions and Compulsions. Englewood Cliffs, NJ, Prentice-Hall, 1980

Rapoport JL, Ryland D, Kriete M: Drug treatment of canine acral lick: an animal model of obsessive-compulsive disorder. Arch Gen Psychiatry 49:517–521, 1992

Rasmussen SA, Eisen JL: Phenomenology of obsessive compulsive disorder, in Psychobiology of Obsessive-Compulsive Disorder. Edited by Insel J, Rasmussen S. New York, Springer-Verlag, 1991, pp 743–758

Rasmussen SA, Tsuang MT: Clinical characteristics and family history in DSM-III obsessive-compulsive disorder. Am J Psychiatry 143:317–322, 1986

Rasmussen SA, Eisen JL, Pato MT: Current issues in the pharmacologic management of obsessive-compulsive disorder. J Clin Psychiatry 54 (6, suppl):4–9, 1993

Rasmussen SA, Goodman WK, Greist JH, et al: Fluvoxamine in the treatment of obsessive compulsive disorder: a multicenter, double-blind placebo-controlled study in outpatients. Am J Psychiatry (in press)

Rauch SL, Jenike MA, Alpert NM, et al: Regional cerebral blood flow measured during symptom provocation in obsessive-compulsive disorder using oxygen 15-labeled carbon dioxide and positron emission tomography. Arch Gen Psychiatry 51:62–70, 1994

Ricciardi JN, Baer L, Jenike MA, et al: Changes in DSM-III-R Axis II diagnoses following treatment of obsessive-compulsive disorder. Am J Psychiatry 149:829–831, 1992

Riddle MA, Scahill L, King R, et al: Obsessive compulsive disorder in children and adolescents: phenomenology and family history. J Am Acad Child Adolesc Psychiatry 29:766–772, 1990

Robertson MM, Trimble MR, Lees AJ: The psychopathology of the Gilles de la Tourette syndrome: a phenomenological analysis. Br J Psychiatry 152:283–390, 1988

Robins LN, Helzer JE, Weissman MM, et al: Lifetime prevalence of specific psychiatric disorders in three sites. Arch Gen Psychiatry 41:958–967, 1984

Rubenstein CS, Pigott TA, L'Heureux F, et al: A preliminary investigation of the lifetime prevalence of anorexia and bulimia nervosa in patients with obsessive compulsive disorder. J Clin Psychiatry 53:309–314, 1992

Schwartz JM, Stoessel PW, Baxter LR, et al: Systematic changes in cerebral glucose metabolic rate after successful behavior modification treatment of obsessive-compulsive disorder. Arch Gen Psychiatry 53:109–113, 1996

Stangl D, Pfohl B, Zimmerman M, et al: A structured interview for the DSM-III personality disorders: preliminary report. Arch Gen Psychiatry 42:591–596, 1985

Swedo SE, Rapoport JL, Leonard H, et al: Obsessive-compulsive disorder in children and adolescents: clinical phenomenology of 70 consecutive cases. Arch Gen Psychiatry 46:335–341, 1989a

Swedo SE, Schapiro MB, Grady CL, et al: Cerebral glucose metabolism in childhood-onset obsessive compulsive disorder. Arch Gen Psychiatry 46:518–523, 1989b

Swedo SE, Pietrini P, Leonard HL, et al: Cerebral glucose metabolism in childhood onset obsessive-compulsive disorder: revisualization during pharmacology. Arch Gen Psychiatry 49:690–694, 1992

Thiel A, Broocks A, Ohlmeier M, et al: Obsessive-compulsive disorder among patients with anorexia nervosa and bulimia nervosa. Am J Psychiatry 152:72–75, 1995

Thorén P, Åsberg M, Bertilsson L, et al: Clomipramine treatment of obsessive compulsive disorder, II: biochemical aspects. Arch Gen Psychiatry 37:1289–1294, 1980

Tollefson GD, Birkett M, Koran L, et al: Continuation treatment of OCD: double-blind and open-label experience with fluoxetine. J Clin Psychiatry 55 (10, suppl):69–76, 1994a

Tollefson GD, Rampey AH, Potvin JH, et al: A multicenter investigation of fixed dose fluoxetine in the treatment of obsessive-compulsive disorder. Arch Gen Psychiatry 51:559–567, 1994b

Wheadon D, Bushnell W, Steiner M: A fixed-dose comparison of 20, 40, or 60 mg paroxetine to placebo in the treatment of obsessive-compulsive disorder. ACNP Annual Meeting, Honolulu, Hawaii, December 1993

Wood A, Tollefson GD, Birkett M: Pharmacotherapy of obsessive compulsive disorder: experience with fluoxetine. Int Clin Psychopharmacol 8:301–306, 1993

World Health Organization: International Classification of Diseases, 10th Revision. Geneva, Switzerland, World Health Organization, 1992

Zohar J, Mueller E, Insel T et al: Serotonergic responsivity in obsessive-compulsive disorder: comparison of patients and healthy controls. Arch Gen Psychiatry 44:946–951, 1987

Chapter 13

Obsessive-Compulsive Disorder in Later Life

C. Alec Pollard, Ph.D., Cheryl N. Carmin, Ph.D., and Raymond Ownby, M.D., Ph.D.

The past decade has witnessed phenomenal growth in the clinical and research literature on obsessive-compulsive disorder (OCD). However, until recently, very little has been written about OCD in the elderly. Although general knowledge about the nature and treatment of OCD has no doubt assisted clinicians working with elderly patients, the applicability of this information to older adults has not been clearly established. Furthermore, information relevant to the elderly is scattered throughout a variety of different sources. In this chapter we review the literature and discuss clinical issues concerning the epidemiology, diagnosis, and treatment of OCD in later life.

Epidemiology and Demographics

It has been more than a decade since large-scale epidemiological studies revealed that OCD affects a significantly larger portion of the general population than was previously assumed (Myers et al. 1984; Robins et al. 1984). Subsequently, more-specific information regarding the prevalence of OCD in the elderly has become available. Although initial onset of OCD is less common in later life (Blazer et al. 1991; Flint 1994), 1- and 6-month prevalence rates of 0.8% (Regier et al. 1988) and 1.5% (Bland et al. 1988; Kolada et al. 1994), respectively, have been reported for OCD in samples of the general population over 65 years old. Somewhat lower OCD rates of 0.0%–0.6% were found in one study that used a different diagnostic method (Copeland et al. 1987a, 1987b). The prevalence of OCD in those who live in institutions, such as nursing homes, is several times greater than that in other elderly persons (Bland et al. 1988; Junginger et al. 1993).

Data regarding the relative morbidity risk of OCD in elderly men and women are inconsistent. Findings from five sites in the United States suggest that elderly men and women are at equal risk for OCD

The authors wish to express their appreciation to Roberto A. Dominguez, M.D., for his comments on an earlier version of this chapter.

(Regier et al. 1988). However, another study conducted in Edmonton, Canada, found prevalence rates of 0.9% and 1.9%, respectively, in elderly males and females, suggesting that morbidity risk is higher for women (Bland et al. 1988). Evidence of a clear association between OCD and other demographic variables in older adult samples has not been reported.

Diagnosis

Diagnostic Criteria and Clinical Presentation

At present there is no reason to believe that DSM-IV (American Psychiatric Association 1994) criteria are not equally applicable to the elderly. To meet criteria for OCD, individuals must have either obsessions or compulsions that cause marked distress or that significantly interfere with their lives. Obsessions are recurrent and persistent thoughts, impulses, or ideas that are experienced as intrusive and inappropriate and that cause marked anxiety or distress. Common themes of obsessions include contamination, harm to oneself or others, sex, and blasphemy. Compulsions are the repetitive behaviors (e.g., hand washing, checking, straightening) or mental acts (e.g., replacing "bad" thoughts with "good" thoughts, praying, counting) a person performs to reduce or otherwise neutralize an obsession or the discomfort associated with it.

It has been suggested that certain specific presentations of OCD are more likely to occur in the elderly. Examples reported by clinicians include obsessions and compulsions related to fear of forgetting names (Jenike 1991), OCD accompanied by bipolar illness (Gordon and Rasmussen 1988), and pronounced ego-syntonic scrupulosity (Fallon et al. 1990). Despite these case examples, there is currently no convincing evidence that particular constellations of obsessions and compulsions are unique to older adults. Typical presentations of OCD, such as contamination fears with washing rituals and fears of harming others accompanied by checking compulsions, are also commonly found in elderly patients (Calamari et al. 1994).

Differential Diagnosis of Medical Disorders

Because of the prominence of anxiety in OCD, consideration should be given during assessment to medical illnesses common in the elderly that can produce or exacerbate anxiety-like symptoms (Gurian and Miner 1991; Markovitz 1993; Shader et al. 1987). The association between anxiety symptoms and disease in almost any organ system is well known but not always well appreciated. Cardiovascular disease, especially such conditions as cardiac arrhythmias or congestive heart failure resulting in shortness of breath, can produce anxiety-like symptoms such as tachycardia and chest pain. Diseases of the respiratory system such as pneumonia or chronic obstructive pulmonary disease (COPD) may manifest as symptoms resembling anxiety, such as difficulty breathing or lightheadedness. Other conditions that can produce symptoms difficult to distinguish from anxiety include endocrinological diseases such as hyper- or hypothyroidism and diabetes mellitus, neurological diseases such as stroke or the degenerative dementias, and use or abuse of certain substances (e.g., alcohol). The myriad illnesses that may mimic or be accompanied by anxiety symptoms make accurate evaluation of the elderly OCD patient imperative. At a minimum, such an evaluation should include a complete medical and psychiatric history, a physical examination that includes a meticulous neurological assessment, and appropriate laboratory studies.

Although these diseases are always important to consider, few of them can be expected to produce the full syndrome of OCD, with the possible exception of a cerebrovascular accident in the area of the basal ganglia (Simpson and Baldwin 1995). It may be best to view OCD in the elderly from a biopsychosocial perspective, wherein medical illnesses, developmental stressors, and social stressors each function in varying degrees as predisposing or exacerbating factors that then interact in combination with premorbid personality, social functioning, and the larger psychosocial environment. From this perspective, the stress of a medical illness may elevate a subclinical pattern of functioning to clinical prominence for the first time in old age. Similarly, removal of an important social support, as may happen with the death of a spouse, might bring an already extant disorder to clinical attention. Following the general principle of trying to maximize functioning in all systems, clinicians treating an older adult with OCD should be concerned with obtaining optimal treatment for all presenting problems. For example, this objective might encompass optimizing treatment for a patient's COPD, providing pharmacological and behavioral treatments for the OCD, intervening in marital discord, and arranging social service support to help the patient deal with third-party payers and other practical issues.

Differential Diagnosis of Psychiatric Disorders

Psychiatric comorbidity in elderly OCD patients does not appear to be substantially different from that found in younger adults. Conditions most commonly accompanying OCD include depression, other anxiety disorders, and DSM Axis II disorders (Steketee et al., in press). Identification of psychiatric comorbidity can have clear implications for treatment. In some cases, for example, treatment of the OCD may need to be delayed until the comorbid condition has been addressed. A severely depressed patient may lack the energy and motivation needed to engage in behavior therapy (Foa et al. 1983). Remediation of the depression can help prepare the patient to begin addressing his or her OCD.

In addition to assessing comorbidity, it is also important to consider psychiatric conditions that sometimes include symptoms appearing to be obsessive-compulsive in nature. Depression, delusional disorders, degenerative dementias, and schizophrenia can all develop late in life, and each can produce persistent obsessive thoughts that resemble OCD. Repetitive behavior that has the appearance of a compulsion can also occur in disorders other than OCD. Stereotyped movements and checking behaviors, for example, are not uncommon in schizophrenia (Berman et al. 1995).

Careful history taking, with information obtained from collateral sources, is critical in understanding the patient's presentation. With adequate information, the clinician can determine whether a patient's excessive concern about having things stolen from his or her home is a symptom of OCD, a continuation of a lifelong pattern of suspiciousness, or the first manifestation of a degenerative dementia. True OCD symptoms can usually be distinguished by their typical presentation (e.g., contamination fears), their long-standing character (with onset early in life), and the relative preservation of reality testing in other areas of the patient's life. Conversely, persistent, unrealistic beliefs characteristic of late-life schizophrenia or delusional disorder are more likely to focus on persecutory themes, whereas such beliefs in depression are usually related to themes of loss.

It is important to keep in mind that OCD may develop de novo late in life, and that any individual elderly patient can present with an unusual pattern of symptoms. There are no inviolable rules for differentiating obsessions or compulsions from similar phenomena in other disorders. The final determination regarding differential diagnosis rests on the skill and thoroughness of the evaluating clinician. Accurate diagnosis requires a clear understanding of the range of presentations of OCD possible in the elderly (Calamari et al. 1994).

Treatment

Pharmacological Intervention

Serotonergic medications such as clomipramine, fluoxetine, fluvoxamine, sertraline, and paroxetine have been effective in improving OCD symptoms (Greist et al. 1995; Piccinelli et al. 1995; Stein et al. 1995). Although controlled trials with older adults are currently not available to guide clinical practice, case reports suggest that these same medications are likely to be as effective in the elderly as they are in younger adults (Austin et al. 1991; Bajulaiye and Addonizio 1993; Shader et al. 1987; Sheikh and Salzman 1995; Stoudemire and Moran 1993). Selection of the appropriate medication for an elderly person with OCD, however, should be based on history of response, adverse side-effect profile, and likely efficacy. For example, although clomipramine is effective in treating OCD in younger persons, its adverse sedative and anticholinergic effects makes it less desirable for use in the elderly.

The clinician initiating pharmacological treatment with geriatric OCD patients must take into account several factors that affect amount and scheduling of dose. Ability to metabolize drugs may diminish with increasing age due to changes in enzyme activity in the liver and reduced clearance of drugs by the kidneys. Body composition also can change with increased age, resulting in a decrease in the ratio of lean muscle to fat. Lipophilic drugs may thus have higher volumes of distribution and slower elimination, so that the activity of some medications may be prolonged. In addition, perhaps due to decreased cognitive reserve, some elderly individuals are more sensitive to the cognitive side effects of medications. Older adults are also more susceptible to adverse drug interactions, a vulnerability compounded by the larger number of medications they are likely to be taking. These facts warrant an approach to pharmacotherapy that begins with careful evaluation of the patient's medical and psychiatric status. The physician should initiate treatment with low doses of medication, maintain vigilance for the emergence of adverse effects, and increase doses slowly.

Considering a medication's potential for adverse effects is extremely important when initiating therapy with the elderly, and the OCD patient is no exception. Assessment of a patient's susceptibility to other anxiety-producing agents, such as caffeine or the pseudoephedrine contained in many cold medications, may help guide the clinician in prescribing low doses of medication and in alerting the patient to possible adverse effects. Although some physicians have expressed concern about increasing an already vigilant patient's awareness of side effects, forewarning patients more often serves as an inoculation procedure. Informed patients are less likely to be surprised by side effects and may be more willing to endure the protracted pharmacological treatment sometimes necessary with OCD.

Although studies have shown that all five of the serotonergic medications available in the United States are effective in treating OCD, a comparison of treatment effect sizes suggests an inverse relationship between serotonergic specificity and amount of symptom improvement (Jenike et al. 1990). Studies thus favor the less serotonin-specific agents such as clomipramine, fluoxetine, and fluvoxamine over the more specific agent sertraline.

Thus, the first-choice treatment for OCD in the elderly might be a low dose of fluoxetine. The dose should then be increased gradually.

Because fluoxetine may initially increase anxiety, therapy with this agent should begin at a low dose (as low as 10 mg/day or lower if needed) that is increased gradually. OCD treatment sometimes requires higher doses of medication than are needed for managing depression. Although doses should be increased cautiously in the elderly, many older persons may ultimately require doses similar to those used to treat younger adults with OCD. Age and health of the person, of course, should also affect dosage decisions. The initial dose of medication for a healthy 65-year-old man might be substantially different from that prescribed for a frail 80-year-old woman. As therapy progresses, dosage changes should be individualized according to clinical response and tolerance of adverse effects.

As is true in the treatment of younger OCD patients, an extended period of therapy may be required. Patients should receive an adequate dose (maximized with respect to treatment response and adverse effects) of medication for at least 10 weeks before a particular drug is determined ineffective. It is useful to supplement a patient's report of therapeutic response to medication with a standardized self-report measure such as the Modified Maudsley Obsessive-Compulsive Inventory (MMOCI; Dominguez et al. 1989) or a therapist rating scale such as the Yale-Brown Obsessive Compulsive Scale (Y-BOCS; Goodman et al. 1989a; Goodman et al. 1989b). If possible, assessment of treatment response should also include reports from family members and other collateral sources familiar with the patient's day-to-day functioning.

Data on alternative strategies for elderly patients with inadequate response to serotonergic monotherapy are virtually nonexistent. Augmentation is one option, but other steps should be considered first. If response to one serotonergic medication is inadequate, it is reasonable to try another. It may even be worthwhile to try a third serotonergic medication before investigating strategies that combine several medications (Dominguez and Mestre 1994). Furthermore, before initiating augmentation, it is useful to thoroughly review the diagnosis, the patient's compliance with therapy, the adequacy of dosing (via blood levels when available), the potential impact of family functioning and life stressors, and the status of the patient's participation in behavior therapy. The importance of participation in behavior therapy cannot be overemphasized. Consideration of the patient's status in behavioral treatment should be an integral part of evaluating response to medication.

After first-line treatments have been fully explored, augmentation with one of the serotonergic medications can be considered. Each augmentation strategy has advantages and disadvantages, and choice of strategy should involve consideration of patient characteristics such as frailty, susceptibility to falls, ability to metabolize the various medications available, and sensitivity to cholinergic effects.

Augmentation strategies targeting serotonergic pathways, such as the use of lithium or buspirone, have been disappointing in small controlled trials. Although lithium is undoubtedly an effective augmentation agent in treating depression, there is little evidence of its effectiveness in augmenting the antiobsessional effects of other serotonergic medications. Because of the risk of toxicity and potential interactions with medications (e.g., antihypertensive and nonsteroidal antiinflammatory drugs) commonly used by the elderly, lithium augmentation should be viewed in most cases as an undesirable approach to augmentation with this population.

An augmentation strategy with minimal risk is to add buspirone to one of the monotherapy agents. The anxiolytic effect of buspirone may improve some patients' functioning even if it does not directly affect OCD symptoms. Buspirone has few adverse effects and is unlikely to impair cognitive or motor functioning in the elderly. It thus appears to be a safe choice for augmentation, although its efficacy with OCD needs to be more clearly demonstrated.

Although clonazepam has been used as an effective augmentation strategy (Dominguez and Mestre 1994), enthusiasm for its use with the elderly must be tempered by its potential to cause excessive sedation and to accumulate in the patient's system over time. Because benzodiazepine use is a risk factor for falls in the elderly, clonazepam should not be prescribed for persons who are frail or who already have gait disturbances. If augmentation with clonazepam is attempted, the clinician should carefully monitor the elderly person's cognitive and motor functioning.

The addition of low doses of a high-potency neuroleptic, such as haloperidol, to a serotonergic medication can be considered with the elderly because of the low likelihood of adverse effects. However, this augmentation strategy is probably most likely to be successful in patients with comorbid tic disorder. Several authors have also described the use of newer atypical neuroleptics alone or in combinations as therapy for OCD (Jacobsen 1995; McDougle et al. 1995). Preliminary data suggest that risperidone may be a useful agent for augmenting the effects of other serotonergic agents (Jacobsen 1995), whereas clozapine is probably not effective as a single-agent treatment for OCD (McDougle et al. 1995). Clinicians treating OCD with clozapine or risperidone should also consider reports suggesting both drugs can exacerbate OCD symptoms (Patel and Tandon 1993; Patil 1992; Remington and Adams 1994).

Very limited evidence exists to support the use of medical interventions other than pharmacotherapy to treat OCD in the elderly. One exception may be the use of cingulotomy and related psychosurgery procedures, which could play a role in the treatment of some highly refractory cases of OCD (Jenike et al. 1991), although data on older adults have not been published. There is one report of the successful use of electroconvulsive therapy (ECT) to treat an 84-year-old woman with a long history of OCD (Casey and Davis 1994). However, both psychosurgery and ECT need to be studied further, specifically with elderly OCD patients.

Psychosocial Intervention

Psychosocial treatment of elderly OCD patients is based largely on research with the general adult population. By far the most consistently effective and well-studied psychological intervention for OCD has been the behavioral treatment known as exposure and response prevention (ERP) (Baer and Minichiello 1990; Dar and Greist 1992; Stanley and Turner 1995; Steketee and Foa 1985). With this procedure, patients are systematically exposed to their obsessions (e.g., contamination) while attempting to resist engaging in compulsions (e.g., washing).

Although ERP is well established as a treatment for OCD in young adults, little has been written on the specific application of this procedure to the elderly (Calamari et al. 1994). King and Barrowclough (1991) have reported success with cognitive-behavioral interventions in a sample of older patients with various anxiety disorders, thus challenging the notion that cognitive deficits of normal aging preclude benefit from psychosocial treatment. Applying behavioral treatments specifically to OCD, several case studies have provided more direct evidence that ERP is effective with elderly patients (Calamari et al. 1994; Junginger and Ditto 1984; Rowan et al. 1984; Turner et al. 1979). Results of one study indicate that older persons with OCD may derive as much benefit from behavioral treatment as do younger OCD patients (Carmin et al. 1995). Ten OCD patients aged 60 and older and 10 younger adult OCD patients matched for sex and clinical severity received ERP. At the end of treatment, both groups had improved, and no significant differences in outcome were found between the older and younger patients. This finding is particularly noteworthy given that the duration of illness reported by the older patients was more than twice that reported by their younger counterparts. Although these reports are promising, more research is needed to clearly establish the exportability of behavioral treatment to the elderly (Hersen and Van Hasselt 1992; McCarthy et al. 1991).

No controlled studies have evaluated modifications of behavior therapy that might be necessary to successfully address the needs of elderly OCD patients. However, the clinical literature and our experience suggest that certain adaptations of treatment are sometimes needed. One important clinical consideration is how physical illness, which is more prevalent in older adults, affects treatment planning and implementation. For example, patients whose treatment for contamination fears could involve touching objects outdoors may be unable to do so during hot, cold, or windy weather if they suffer from severe or poorly controlled angina. Similarly, the pace of exposure will need to be reduced for patients with emphysema who require supplemental oxygen and are unable to engage in more than limited physical exertion. Clinicians treating the medically compromised elderly must be adept at suspending, reinitiating, and modifying behavior therapy as needed in response to medical complications.

Nonphysician behavior therapists working with elderly OCD patients should familiarize themselves with side-effect and drug-interaction profiles of medications such as the serotonin reuptake inhibitors. Age-related changes in response to some medications and increased medical comorbidity mean greater potential for drug interactions. Behavior therapists often see patients more frequently than do other clinicians and should thus be observant for medication problems that need to be communicated to the patient's physician. When patients are seen by multiple specialists, collaborative case management is even more important. To begin with, it is crucial that elderly patients are medically cleared for behavioral treatment and that the physician understands what this form of therapy involves. A collaborative approach provides a safeguard for the therapist in terms of the interaction of treatment strategies with the patient's medical condition and helps prevent patients from inappropriately using their medical problems as a reason to avoid behavioral interventions. In turn, the therapist may be able to assist physicians in addressing behavioral problems that complicate the patient's medical treatment.

In addition to increased medical comorbidity, normal aging is associated with some limitations in physical and cognitive agility that can affect treatment. ERP, for example, may need to be modified. This intervention ordinarily involves experiencing modest to high levels of anxiety, and the attenuated stamina of some older patients can dissuade them from pursuing behavior therapy. Pacing treatment judiciously helps prevent some patients from becoming overwhelmed. On the other hand, some patients will resist pacing because they perceive it as a concession to their advancing age. The speed at which treatment progresses and the level of difficulty of the ERP regimen need to be discussed regularly in therapy to help prevent patients from becoming unnecessarily discouraged or overwhelmed.

Just as reduced stamina presents a challenge to treatment, so, too, can the presence of physical disability. Treatment strategies sometimes need to be tailored to accommodate sensory or motor impairment. It is also important to differentiate OCD symptoms from compensatory behaviors related to impairment. For example, a patient who repeatedly asks if a chair looks clean enough to sit on could be compulsively seeking reassurance or might simply be compensating for poor vision. Sometimes interventions like a hearing aid, glasses, or cataract surgery clarify the nature of the behavior. Non-OCD impairments that interfere with treatment but cannot be corrected may still need to be addressed in order to administer therapy successfully. For example, using audiotaped descriptions of exposure scenes to administer imaginal flooding will be of little value to a patient who is hearing impaired. In this situation, creative use of written or videotaped material may be necessary for adequate exposure.

Elderly individuals are also more vulnerable to decline in cognitive functions such as memory (Lindesay et al. 1989), which presents an assessment challenge similar to that involved in evaluating sensory and motor impairment. The clinician needs to discern whether ritualistic behavior is, in fact, a compulsion or an adaptation to offset cognitive deficits. Repetitive checking, placement, and list-making behaviors can all serve as memory aids in certain individuals. Although the presence of mild to moderate memory deficits in addition to OCD symptoms does not obviate behavioral treatment, adaptations sometimes need to be made. For example, failure to remember the principles of response prevention will seriously threaten the success of behavior therapy in OCD. However, written reminders to resist rituals can be strategically placed within the patient's environment as aids to help ensure proper adherence to the response prevention protocol.

General Treatment Considerations

In addition to factors specifically related to pharmacological or behavioral treatment, other general clinical issues and practical obstacles exist that can complicate the management of OCD in elderly patients. In this section we discuss additional treatment considerations relevant to the geriatric OCD patient.

Circumventing resistance to treatment.   Although the stigma of having OCD has certainly not vanished, older adults grew up in a society in which having a psychiatric condition was considered more shameful than it is today. Not surprisingly, many elderly patients are reluctant to acknowledge their problem and to seek help (German et al. 1985; Himmelfarb and Murrell 1984). Extra time may need to be devoted to preparing older patients to engage in treatment. For the elder who refuses help altogether, family counseling is sometimes the first step. Whether working with patients or their families, it is important that clinicians respect the values and cultural background of their older patients.

Sometimes reluctance to engage in treatment comes from a culture-bound belief that, unlike medical disorders, psychiatric problems reflect a weakness in intelligence or moral character. It is therefore not unusual for patients to focus on some other illness or the "medical" aspects of their OCD. Rather than attempting to persuade the patient to assume a biopsychosocial model of OCD, the clinician may find it more helpful initially to adopt the patient's model and then to gradually introduce the importance of managing behavioral aspects of disease. Management of medical conditions such as diabetes and hypertension can be used as an illustration of the role behavioral interventions can play in the treatment of OCD.

Resistance may also be reflected in a patient's reluctance to use contemporary mental health language. In such cases, the clinician can adopt language meaningful to the patient. For example, some older patients do not like the word *anxiety,* either because its meaning is less familiar or because the word has a negative connotation for them. Use of another word, such as "nervous" or "distressed," might be more readily accepted. Some patients are unable or reluctant to rate their distress levels with numeric scales like the Subjective Units of Disturbance Scale (SUDS; Wolpe 1973). In such cases, it is sometimes helpful to adopt a more acceptable alternative method by asking patients simply to rate their anxiety level as high, medium, or low.

Dealing with family issues.   Although family intervention is not always necessary, it is usually helpful. Recent evidence that family behavior is related to level of functioning in OCD patients (Calvocoressi et al. 1995) has confirmed what many clinicians have long suspected. The more OCD patients interact with or are dependent upon spouses, children, and other relatives, the greater the need for family intervention. In many ways, the goals of intervening with families of older individuals are similar to those of dealing with families of younger adults. The aim is to correct misinformation and negative stereotypes about OCD, teach ways to support the patient's recovery, and help family members reduce behavior that can impede the patient's progress. The therapist tries to help them learn that responding to the patient by being overly critical, accommodating rituals, or providing repeated reassurances will only exacerbate the patient's condition.

There are a few family-related issues that clinicians working with older individuals are especially likely to encounter. In many instances, the therapist is working with the patient's adult children, who may be grappling with a shift in the nature of their relationship to the OCD patient. Because of limitations in the patient's functioning imposed by OCD or other infirmities associated with aging, the adult children may have assumed more of a parental or custodial role. Extra attention may need to be devoted in family sessions to facilitation of this often awkward and uncomfortable reversal of roles. Under these circumstances, issues of patient confidentiality and family boundaries are in many ways similar to those involved in working with the families of children and adolescents.

Consulting to residential and home healthcare personnel. Although many older OCD patients are otherwise physically and mentally healthy, some require regular contact with caregivers such as nursing home staff or home healthcare providers. To the extent that these individuals interact with and thus have the opportunity to influence the behavior of the OCD patient, it is important to involve them in treatment. Objectives of involving caregivers in treatment are largely the same as those of including family members. For practical and therapeutic reasons, it may be necessary for the therapist to consult with caregivers at the patient's residence, a practice that is admittedly not routine for many clinicians. However, the positive impact of involving key individuals in therapy is worth the extra effort of coordinating a home visit with that of the home healthcare professional. When the patient lives in a nursing home, it is helpful to meet with as many of the relevant staff as possible. The change of shift, usually occurring in the late afternoon, is often a good time to catch day and evening personnel together. Although it is beneficial to educate as many staff members as possible, it also helps to identify a primary individual to serve as liaison with the rest of the staff.

Addressing stressors and fears common in later life. Each developmental stage has its own unique challenges for obsessive-compulsive individuals (Francis and Borden 1993). Although there is little evidence of an OCD presentation unique to older adults, clinicians should be aware of stressors and fears common in later life that could influence the course of the disorder (Patterson 1988). Certain major life events, such as death of a spouse, onset or development of physical illness or disability, or relocation to a retirement or nursing home, are more likely to occur in later life. Such stressors can contribute to relapse in recovered individuals, and may also play a role in the development of late-life-onset OCD. Assisting patients to address life stressors can have a positive effect on OCD symptoms. At the very least, it is helpful for patients to understand the factors that exacerbate their condition.

Some fears are more common than others in later life. On the one hand, the elderly are often less worried than younger adults about social threats such as rejection or criticism (Wisocki 1994). However, infirmity, loss of mobility and independence, and becoming a burden to loved ones are common worries during this phase of life (Wisocki 1994). The elderly are also more prone to fears of falling. Typically, a fall may involve surgical intervention with all of the attendant concerns that hospitalization and recovery imply. The emergence of such fears can add to the patient's overall anxiety and can indirectly exacerbate OCD symptoms or interfere with treatment. Each case must be considered individually, but it is sometimes necessary to treat significant comorbid fears along with or before treating OCD symptoms.

Monitoring relapse.   Cognitive decline can be confounded with the symptoms of relapse. The first evidence of memory problems associated with dementia, for example, might appear to be compulsive reassurance-seeking. Alternatively, OCD-related behaviors should not be dismissed as age-related when, in fact, they could be signaling impending relapse. The therapist working with an elderly patient must be sensitive to both sides of this complex issue. It is generally advisable to set up a regular schedule of maintenance visits after the patient has completed therapy. The patient, family members, and caregivers should also be informed of the principles of relapse prevention.

Conclusions

There is preliminary evidence that established pharmacological and behavioral treatments for OCD are beneficial for older adults with this disorder. Nonetheless, guidelines for the clinical management of OCD in elderly patients are still based in large part on research conducted in samples of younger adults. Practitioners providing care to older individuals with OCD are encouraged to be cognizant of clinical issues particularly relevant to this phase of adulthood. Diagnostic and treatment procedures may need to be modified to attend to the physical, psychological, and social complications that can emerge in later life. Further research is needed to fully establish the safety and efficacy of serotonergic medications, ERP, and other interventions used to treat late-life OCD. It will also be important to determine when and how to adapt these interventions to effectively address clinical challenges associated with treating OCD in the elderly.

References

American Psychiatric Association: Diagnostic and Statistical Manual of Mental Disorders, 4th Edition. Washington, DC, American Psychiatric Association, 1994

Austin LS, Zealberg JJ, Lydiard RB: Three cases of pharmacotherapy of obsessive-compulsive disorder in the elderly. J Nerv Ment Dis 179:634–635, 1991

Baer L, Minichiello WE: Behavior therapy for obsessive-compulsive disorder, in Obsessive-Compulsive Disorders: Theory and Management, 2nd Edition. Edited by Jenike MA, Baer L, Minichiello WE. Chicago, IL, Year Book Medical, 1990, pp 203–232

Bajulaiye R, Addonizio G: Obsessive-compulsive disorder arising in a 75-year-old woman. International Journal of Geriatric Psychiatry 7:139–142, 1993

Berman I, Kalinowski A, Berman SM, et al: Obsessive and compulsive symptoms in chronic schizophrenia. Compr Psychiatry 36:6–10, 1995

Bland RC, Newman SC, Orn H: Prevalence of psychiatric disorders in the elderly in Edmonton. Acta Psychiatric Scand Suppl 338:57–63, 1988

Blazer D, George LK, Hughes D: The epidemiology of anxiety disorders: an age comparison, in Anxiety in the Elderly: Treatment and Research. Edited by Salzman C, Lebowitz BD. New York, Springer, 1991, pp 17–30

Calamari JE, Faber SD, Hitsman BL, et al: Treatment of obsessive compulsive disorder in the elderly: a review and case example. Journal of Behavior Therapy and Experimental Psychiatry 25:95–104, 1994

Calvocoressi L, Lewis BL, Harris J, et al: Family accommodations in obsessive-compulsive disorder. Am J Psychiatry 152:441–443, 1995

Carmin CN, Pollard CA, Ownby RL: Effects of cognitive behavioral treatment of obsessive-compulsive disorder in geriatric vs. younger adult patients. Paper presented at the 29th annual convention of the Association for the Advancement of Behavior Therapy, Washington, DC, November 1995

Casey DA, Davis MH: Obsessive-compulsive disorder responsive to electroconvulsive therapy in an elderly woman. Southern Medical Journal 87:862–864, 1994

Copeland JRM, Dewey ME, Wood N, et al: Range of mental illness among the elderly in the community: prevalence in Liverpool using the GMS-AGECAT package. Br J Psychiatry 150:815–823, 1987a

Copeland JRM, Garland BJ, Dewey ME, et al: Is there more dementia, depression and neurosis in New York? a comparative study of the elderly in New York and London using the computer diagnosis AGECAT. Br J Psychiatry 151:466–473, 1987b

Dar R, Greist JH: Behavior therapy for obsessive compulsive disorder. Psychiatr Clin North Am 15:885–894, 1992

Dominguez RA, Mestre SM: Management of treatment-refractory obsessive compulsive disorder patients. J Clin Psychiatry 55 (suppl):86–92, 1994

Dominguez RA, Jacobson AF, Del Gandra J, et al: Drug response assessed by the Modified Maudsley Obsessive-Compulsive Inventory. Psychopharmacol Bull 25:215–218, 1989

Fallon BA, Liebowitz MR, Hollander E, et al: The pharmacotherapy of moral or religious scrupulosity. J Clin Psychiatry 51:517–521, 1990

Flint AJ: Epidemiology and comorbidity of anxiety disorders in the elderly. Am J Psychiatry 151:640–649, 1994

Foa EB, Steketee GS, Grayson JB, et al: Treatment of obsessive-compulsives: when do we fail? in Failures in Behavior Therapy. Edited by Emmelkamp PMG. New York, Wiley, 1983, pp 10–34

Francis G, Borden J: Expression and treatment of obsessive-compulsive disorder in childhood, adolescence, and adulthood, in Anxiety Across the Lifespan: A Developmental Perspective. Edited by Last C. New York, Springer, 1993, pp 148–166

German PS, Shapiro S, Skinner EA: Mental health of the elderly: use of health and mental health services. J Am Geriatr Soc 33:246–252, 1985

Goodman WK, Price L, Rasmussen S, et al: The Yale-Brown Obsessive Compulsive Scale, I: development, use, and reliability. Arch Gen Psychiatry 46:1006–1011, 1989a

Goodman, WK, Price L, Rasmussen S, et al: The Yale-Brown Obsessive Compulsive Scale, II: validity. Arch Gen Psychiatry 46:1012–1016, 1989b

Gordon A, Rasmussen SA: Mood-related obsessive compulsive symptoms in a patient with bipolar affective disorder. J Clin Psychiatry 49:27–28, 1988

Greist JM, Jefferson JW, Kobak KH, et al: Efficacy and tolerability of serotonin transport inhibitors in obsessive-compulsive disorder: a meta-analysis. Arch Gen Psychiatry 52:53–60, 1995

Gurian BS, Miner JH: Clinical presentation of anxiety in the elderly, in Anxiety in the Elderly: Treatment and Research. Edited by Salzman C, Lebowitz BD. New York, Springer, 1991, pp 31–44

Hersen M, Van Hasselt VB: Behavioral assessment and treatment of anxiety in the elderly. Clinical Psychology Review 12:619–640, 1992

Himmelfarb S, Murrell SA: The prevalence and correlation of anxiety symptoms in older adults. J Psychology 116:159–167, 1984

Jacobsen FM: Risperidone in the treatment of affective illness and obsessive-compulsive disorder. J Clin Psychiatry 56:423–429, 1995

Jenike MA: Geriatric obsessive compulsive disorder. Geriatric Psychiatry and Neurology 4:34–39, 1991

Jenike MA, Baer L, Ballentine HT, et al: Cingulotomy for refractory obsessive-compulsive disorder. Arch Gen Psychiatry 48:548–555, 1991

Jenike MA, Hyman S, Baer L, et al: A controlled trial of fluvoxamine in obsessive-compulsive disorder: implications for serotonergic theory. Am J Psychiatry 147:1209–1215, 1990

Junginger J, Ditto B: Multitreatment of obsessive-compulsive checking in a geriatric patient. Behavior Modification 8:379–390, 1984

Junginger J, Phelan E, Cherry K, et al: Prevalence of psychopathology in elderly persons in nursing homes and in the community. Hospital and Community Psychiatry 44:381–383, 1993

King P, Barrowclough C: A clinical pilot study of cognitive-behavioral therapy for anxiety disorders in the elderly. Behavioral Psychotherapy 19:337–345, 1991

Kolada JL, Bland RC, Newman SC: Obsessive-compulsive disorder. Acta Psychiatr Scand 376 (suppl):24–35, 1994

Lindesay J, Briggs K, Murphy E: The Guys/Age Concern Survey: prevalence rates of cognitive impairment, depression, and anxiety in an urban elderly community. Br J Psychiatry 155:317–329, 1989

Markovitz PJ: Treatment of anxiety in the elderly. J Clin Psychiatry 54 (suppl):64–68, 1993

McCarthy PR, Katz IR, Foa EB: Cognitive-behavioral treatment of anxiety in the elderly: a proposed model, in Anxiety in the Elderly: Treatment and Research. Edited by Salzman C, Lebowitz BD. New York, Springer, 1991, pp 197–214

McDougle CJ, Barr LC, Goodman WK, et al: Lack of efficacy of clozapine monotherapy in refractory obsessive-compulsive disorder. Am J Psychiatry 152:1812–1814, 1995

Myers JK, Weisman MM, Tischler GL, et al: Six-month prevalence of psychiatric disorders in three communities. Arch Gen Psychiatry 41:959–967, 1984

Patel B, Tandon R: Development of obsessive-compulsive symptoms during clozapine treatment (letter). Am J Psychiatry 150:836, 1993

Patil VJ: Development of transient obsessive-compulsive symptoms during treatment with clozapine (letter). Am J Psychiatry 149:272, 1992

Patterson RL: Anxiety in the elderly, in Handbook of Anxiety Disorders. Edited by Last CG, Hersen M. Elmsford, NY, Pergamon, 1988, pp 541–551

Piccinelli M, Pini S, Bellantuono C, et al: Efficacy of drug treatment in obsessive-compulsive disorder: a meta-analytic review. Br J Psychiatry 36:6–10, 1995

Regier DA, Boyd JH, Burke JD, et al: One-month prevalence of mental disorder in the United States. Arch Gen Psychiatry 45:977–986, 1988

Remington D, Adams M: Risperidone and obsessive compulsive symptoms. J Clin Psychopharmacol 14:358–359, 1994

Robins LN, Helzer JE, Weissman MM, et al: Lifetime prevalence of specific psychiatric disorders in three sites. Arch Gen Psychiatry 41:958–967, 1984

Rowan VC, Holburn W, Walker JR, et al: A rapid multi-component treatment for an obsessive-compulsive disorder. Journal of Behavior Therapy and Experimental Psychiatry 15:347–352, 1984

Shader RI, Kennedy JS, Greenblatt DJ: Treatment of anxiety in the elderly, in Psychopharmacology: The Third Generation of Progress. Edited by Meltzer HY. New York, Raven, 1987, pp 1141–1147

Sheikh JL, Salzman C: Anxiety in the elderly. Psychiatr Clin North Am 18:871–883, 1995

Simpson S, Baldwin B: Neuropsychiatry and SPECT of an acute obsessive-compulsive syndrome patient. Br J Psychiatry 166:390–392, 1995

Stanley MA, Turner SM: Current status of pharmacological and behavioral treatment of obsessive-compulsive disorder. Behavior Therapy 26:163–186, 1995

Stein DJ, Spadacini E, Hollander E: Meta-analysis of pharmacotherapy trials for obsessive-compulsive disorder. Int Clin Psychopharmacol 10:11–18, 1995

Steketee G, Foa EB: Obsessive-compulsive disorder, in Handbook of Clinical Disorders. Edited by Barlow DH. New York, Guilford, 1985, pp 69–144

Steketee G, Heninger N, Pollard CA: Predicting treatment outcome for OCD: effects of comorbidity, in Treatment-Refractory Obsessive-Compulsive Disorder. Edited by Goodman WK, Maser J, Rudorfer M. Mahwah, NJ, Lawrence Erlbaum (in press)

Stoudemire A, Moran MG: Psychopharmacologic treatment of anxiety in the medically ill elderly patient: special considerations. J Clin Psychiatry 54 (suppl):27–33, 1993

Turner SM, Hersen M, Bellack AS, et al: Behavioral treatment of obsessive compulsive neurosis. Behaviour Research and Therapy 17:95–106, 1979

Wisocki PA: The experience of worry among the elderly, in Worrying: Perspectives on Theory, Assessment and Treatment. Edited by Davey GCL, Tallis F. New York, Wiley, 1994, pp 247–261

Wolpe J: The Practice of Behavior Therapy, 2nd Edition. New York, Pergamon, 1973

Chapter 14

Course of Illness in Obsessive-Compulsive Disorder

Jane Eisen, M.D., and Gail Steketee, Ph.D.

Until the mid-1980s, obsessive-compulsive disorder (OCD) was thought to be a rare psychiatric illness. With the use of more sophisticated epidemiological techniques to determine prevalence, OCD is now considered to be a common psychiatric disorder with a lifetime prevalence of 2.5% (Karno et al. 1988). Demographic, epidemiologic, and clinical features of OCD have been well characterized (Rasmussen and Eisen 1992). However, little is known about the course of the disorder over time in terms of patterns of remission and relapse or about factors that may affect illness course, such as age at onset, severity of illness, treatment, comorbidity with Axis I and/or II disorders, and symptom subtypes.

DSM-IV (American Psychiatric Association 1994) describes the course of OCD as typically chronic with some fluctuation in the severity of symptoms over time. Although terminology and definitions vary from study to study, overall, this chronic fluctuating course appears to be supported both retrospectively before treatment and in follow-up after treatment. Early phenomenological and follow-up studies of OCD suffered from a number of methodological limitations, including retrospective study design; small sample sizes; lack of standardized criteria for determining diagnosis; use of hospital-based samples not representative of the spectrum of the disorder found in the population as a whole; biases in inclusion and exclusion criteria; use of chart review rather than personal interview, absence of structured interviews, and lack of consensus on the definition of relapse, remission, and recovery. Because of these flaws in study design, the earlier studies of OCD may have included subjects who would not meet today's criteria. In particular, clear distinctions between OCD and obsessive-compulsive personality disorder (OCPD) were often not made, and obsessions and compulsions occurring in the context of other disorders (e.g., major depression, psychosis, eating disorders) may have been included as OCD.

More recent studies using a prospective design and standardized criteria have also shown that episodicity in this disorder (with clear periods of complete remission off medication) is uncommon. Once established, obsessions and compulsions usually persist, although the content, intensity, and frequency of these symptoms change over time.

In this chapter we review early and more recent findings regarding the course of OCD and then turn our attention to predictors of course. Because data on course inevitably overlap with treatment outcome findings, we also review factors that predict medication and behavioral treatment outcome.

Retrospective Follow-Up Studies

In retrospective studies, fluctuations in the severity of psychiatric symptoms and their impact on functioning over time are ascertained based on subjects' recall. Several investigators have identified patterns of course of illness in OCD as falling into the following categories: complete remission of obsessions and compulsions, symptoms much improved, minimal improvement with poor functioning, and symptoms unchanged or worsening. In these studies, it is often unclear whether patients described as "much improved" would nevertheless still meet criteria for the disorder. Another approach has been to determine the episodicity of a patient's OCD—that is, whether the OCD is characterized by distinct periods of illness and remission, similar to major depressive disorder. Such follow-up studies are compared in Table 14–1, although readers should bear in mind that different measures were used to assign patients into categories of course of illness. For the sake of comparison in Table 14–1, subjects considered to be mildly improved but with poor functioning were combined with subjects whose symptoms were classified as minimally improved, unchanged, or worse.

In the majority of studies described in this section, patients were selected based on chart review and were subsequently assessed at the time of the study either in person or through questionnaires. In the earliest longitudinal study of OCD, a relatively good outcome was observed by Lewis (1936), who followed 50 OCD patients (most of whom received some psychotherapy) at least 5 years after initial assessment. Among this group, 32% were symptom-free, 14% were "much improved," and 44% were minimally improved, unchanged, or worse. Only 10% had followed an episodic course marked by later recurrence after remission. When Pollitt (1957) followed 67 nonleucotomized individuals for a mean of 3.4 years, 24% were symptom-free (similar to the results with psychotherapy), 36% had mild symptoms and were functioning well, and 12% were improved but had impaired functioning. Only 25% reported no change or more severe symptoms than at baseline. This study was somewhat unusual because the majority of patients were selected from an outpatient practice. This selection may explain the better outcome in this study in comparison with other studies that assessed only inpatients. Longer duration of illness at initial evaluation was associated with poorer outcome with respect to severity of symp-

Table 14–1.   Retrospective follow-up studies of obsessive-compulsive disorder (OCD)

Author	N	Mean follow-up (years)	Well (%)	Much improved (%)	Minimally improved, unchanged, or worse (%)	Comments
Lewis (1936)	50	>5	32	14	44	10% episodic course
Pollitt (1957)	67[a]	3.4	24	36	37	Mostly outpatients
Ingram (1961)	29	5.9	7	21[b]	72	Inpatients
Kringlen (1965)	80	13–20	0	24	76	Inpatients
Grimshaw (1965)	100	5	40	24	35	Inpatients
Lo (1967)	88	3.9	23	50	27	In- and outpatients, diagnostic heterogeneity
Coryell (1981)	44	0.5+	8	20	8	Inpatients
Thomsen (1995)	47	6–22	28	47[c]	25	Childhood OCD

[a] nonleucotomized. [b] 1 patient nonleucotomized; 5 patients leucotomized. [c] 26% had subclinical OCD at follow-up, and 21% had episodic course with partial or complete remission between episodes.

toms at follow-up, as might be expected. Duration of illness was also a predictor of course of illness in a study of 29 inpatients with obsessional symptoms whom Ingram (1961) followed for 6 years. In this study, only 21% of the patients were much improved; 72% were minimally improved but functioning poorly, unchanged, or worse. Seven of the 8 patients with much improvement or complete remission of symptoms received leucotomies.

In a study characterized by a long follow-up period, Kringlen (1965) found that at 13–20 years after initial contact, only 24% of the subjects were much improved, whereas 34% described slight improvement in obsessive-compulsive (OC) symptoms, and the largest group, 42%, were unimproved or worse. The patients included in this study were all hospitalized for the first time and may have had severe symptoms, thus contributing to poorer outcome in this study. Somewhat better results were reported in another retrospective follow-up study of inpatients: Grimshaw (1965) assessed 100 inpatients an average of 5 years after discharge. 40% were recovered or only slightly symptomatic, 24% had improved moderately, and 35% remained unchanged or had worsened. Improvements were not associated with any particular treatment.

Lo (1967), in a study conducted in China, also had more optimistic results. He followed 88 patients diagnosed with OCD for a mean of 3.9 years and found 23% symptom-free and 50% with symptoms much improved. This study also followed both in- and outpatients. Patients followed for more than 4 years after initially presenting for treatment were more often found symptom-free (14 of 52, 40%) than were those followed for shorter intervals (4 of 35, 8%). There was clearly some diagnostic heterogeneity in this cohort of patients. More than half the patients had distinct obsessions and compulsions. However, 10% had prominent affective symptoms, and 31% were described as having "phobic and ruminative symptoms" with minimal compulsions. It appears, then, that some of the patients who were in remission at follow-up may have had major depression with obsessional or ruminative thinking during their index episode.

The subsequent occurrence of other psychiatric disorders following onset of OCD has been evaluated. Several investigators have found a relatively high rate of development of schizophrenia, ranging from 6% to 8% (Ingram 1961; Kringlen 1965). By contrast, schizophrenia was seen less frequently in several other studies (Lo 1967; Pollitt 1957; Rosenberg 1968). Lack of standardized diagnostic criteria, leading to the inclusion of depression with psychotic features as schizophrenia, may have contributed to the range of schizophrenia found in these earlier studies. Another factor involved may have been patients' degree of insight regarding their obsessions and compulsions. Patients described as having periods of losing insight into the irrationality of their obsessions and as losing resistance were characterized as being "doubtfully schizophrenic" in several studies. The inclusion of these patients may also have led to a higher frequency of schizophrenia in follow-up studies.

In reviewing these follow-up studies, Goodwin et al. (1969) concluded that the course of OCD is usually chronic but variable, with fluctuations in severity of symptoms. He described depression as being the most common psychiatric disorder to develop after the onset of OCD, and noted that subsequent development of schizophrenia is rare if that disorder is adequately excluded at baseline. In follow-up studies conducted since 1980, criteria used to evaluate course of illness have been different from those used in the earlier studies described previously. Patients have been retrospectively assigned to categories such as "continuous," "waxing and waning," "deteriorative," and "episodic with full remissions between episodes." Rasmussen and Tsuang (1986) conducted a study in which patients were selected based on current enrollment in an outpatient OCD clinic. OCD course among the 44 patients in the study was described as chronic or "continuous" for the vast majority (84%), deteriorating for a few (14%), and episodic for only 1 (2%). The average duration of illness at time of assessment was more than 15 years, again suggesting the chronicity of this disorder. Because these subjects were selected through the process of clinic referral and prospective follow-up was not conducted, no former OCD patients who had already recovered and remained well were included. Patients who developed other major psychiatric disorders such as schizophrenia were also unlikely to be represented in this cohort of clinic patients. In a more recent study of 53 OCD outpatients, Gojer and associates (1987) found a primarily deteriorating course in a surprising 66%, with only 11% remaining the same, 17% fluctuating, 2% improving, and 4% not identifiable.

Two studies have compared control groups with an OCD cohort. Coryell (1981) compared course of illness following hospitalization in 44 patients with OCD versus inpatients with major depression. He observed that although 56% of the patients with OCD demonstrated some improvement at follow-up, this cohort was significantly less likely to experience remission after discharge (22%) than was the comparison cohort of depressed patients (64%). However, suicide occurred significantly less frequently in the cohort of patients with OCD compared with patients with depression.

In a cross-sectional follow-up study, Thomsen (1995) interviewed 47 patients with OCD 6–22 years after they had been treated for OCD as children and compared their characteristics with those of a group of non-OCD psychiatric control subjects. All subjects were at least 18 years old at the time of the follow-up interview. The majority of subjects had either no OCD symptoms (28%) or only subclinical OC symptoms (26%)

at follow-up. Ten subjects (21%) had a chronic course of OCD. This study also assessed outcome by using the Global Assessment Scale (GAS; Endicott et al. 1976). Although findings were not statistically significant, males with childhood-onset OCD appeared to have a poorer outcome than females: 9 of the 10 subjects with GAS scores below 50 at follow-up were males.

More recently, studies have used the Yale-Brown Obsessive Compulsive Scale (Y-BOCS; Goodman et al. 1989)—a scale designed to measure the severity of OC symptoms—to assign patients into groups by percentage of improvement. A recent follow-up study conducted in Austria used structured interviews to assess 62 inpatients who met *International Classification of Diseases,* Ninth Revision (ICD-9; World Health Organization 1977) criteria for OCD (Demal et al. 1993) (see Table 14–2). This study's findings were consistent with those of earlier studies: episodic course with complete remission (11%), episodic with partial remission (24%), deteriorative (10%), continuous and unchanging (27%), and continuous with improvement (24%). The authors found that 29% of the patients had Y-BOCS scores in the normal range, 21% had scores in the "subclinical" range (8–15), and 50% had scores in the clinical range (16–40).

Synthesizing methodologically varied studies, some of which present an optimistic picture and others a pessimistic one, may require more careful examination of reported outcomes. It may be important to separate the best possible outcomes ("full remission" or "symptom free") from those described as "much improved" or "improved," which may indicate persistent symptoms in the abatement phase of a chronic waxing and waning illness. The episodic pattern of full remission (and sometimes later recurrence) appears to occur in about 10%–15% of OCD patients, although this proportion may increase somewhat as follow-up is extended for several years and may also be greater in childhood OCD (Apter and Tyano 1988), in which improvement can be rapid even without treatment (Berman 1942). In most studies, with the notable exception of Gojer et al. (1987), a smaller proportion of OCD patients (6%–14%) seem to follow a deteriorating course. The majority presumably have a course marked by chronicity, with some symptom fluctuation over time but without clear-cut remissions or deterioration.

Several studies in both adults and children with OCD have observed that patients typically have multiple obsessions and compulsions at any given time and that the content of their concerns changes over time (Hanna 1995; Rasmussen and Eisen 1992; Rettew et al. 1992; Swedo et al. 1989). In their study of childhood OCD, Rettew et al. (1992) reported that 85% of their subjects had experienced some change in symptom patterns over time, and usually had more than one type of obsession and compulsion concurrently. Content of obsessions did not seem to be related to developmental stage. In subjects with very early-onset

Table 14–2. Obsessive-compulsive disorder follow-up studies using the Yale-Brown Obsessive Compulsive Scale (Y-BOCS) as the outcome measure

Author	N	Normal range Y-BOCS 0–7 (%)	Subclinical range Y-BOCS 8–15 (%)	Clinical range Y-BOCS 16–40 (%)	Methodology
Demal et al. 1993	62	29.1	20.9	50	Cross-sectional
Orloff et al. 1994	85				Percentage improvement did not allow estimates
Eisen et al. 1995b	65	16.9	35.4	47.7	Prospective

illness (before age 6), symptoms often started with a solitary ritual without associated obsessive thoughts. New symptoms arose that would sometimes become predominant over earlier ones. The factors involved in changes in focus of OC symptoms over time have yet to be delineated. Thus far, symptom subtype has not been found to be a predictor of either illness course or treatment response (see "Predictors of Course," later in this chapter).

Prospective Studies

Over the past decade, several studies of course of illness in childhood-onset OCD have used a prospective design. In one of these studies, all students in a high school were screened for the presence of obsessions and/or compulsions (Flament et al. 1988). Fifty-nine adolescents out of 5,596 high school students screened (1%) were identified as having OCD, subclinical OCD, other psychiatric disorders with OC symptoms, or OCPD. This subgroup was subsequently reinterviewed 2 years after the initial interview by raters blind to the baseline diagnosis (Berg et al. 1989). Of the 12 subjects initially diagnosed with OCD, only 5 still met full criteria for the disorder; 2 had developed OCPD and 3 had other disorders with some obsessional features. The 1 subject who was diagnosed with OCD at baseline but with subclinical OCD at the 2-year interview can be considered analogous to subjects described in other studies as much improved or in partial remission (see Table 14–3). Only 1 subject originally diagnosed with OCD had no diagnosis after 2 years. Of interest is the development of psychiatric symptoms in the 15 students who had subclinical OCD at baseline: at follow-up, 4 met full criteria for OCD, 4 continued to have subclinical OCD, 4 developed other psychiatric disorders with OC features, 1 had OCPD, and only 1 subject had no diagnosis.

Another study prospectively assessed 25 children with OCD 2–7 years after initial evaluation (Flament et al. 1990). Although the majority of subjects (68%) still met criteria for OCD at follow-up, 28% were considered completely well, with no obsessions or compulsions. More than half of the subjects had a lifetime history of major depression, and 44% had another anxiety disorder in addition to OCD, such as social phobia or separation anxiety. Five patients had OCPD, and two patients developed psychotic symptoms (diagnosed as atypical psychosis or schizophreniform disorder).

Over the past few years, several longitudinal naturalistic studies have also been conducted in which adults with OCD were followed prospectively. In one such study, data were collected on course of illness in 68 subjects over a 2-year period (Eisen et al. 1995a). Two instruments were used to evaluate severity of symptoms: the Y-BOCS and the Psy-

Table 14-3. Prospective follow-up studies of obsessive-compulsive disorder (OCD)

Author	Treatments	N	Mean follow-up (years)	Remained in episode (%)	Partial remission (%)	Full remission (%)	Comments
Children and adolescents							
Berg et al. 1989		12	2	42	17[a]	8	17% had compulsive personality or traits
Leonard et al. 1993	SSRIs, BT, psychotherapy, family therapy	54	3.4	43	46	11[b]	70% on medication at follow-up
Adults							
Orloff et al. 1994[c]	SSRIs, BT	85	2.1			33	
Eisen et al. 1995b	SSRIs, BT	51	2	57	31	12	
G. Steketee, J. Eisen, I. Dyck, M. Warshaw, S. Rasmussen, "Predictors of Course of OCD" (submitted for publication)	SSRIs, BT	107	0.5–5	47	31	22	Mainly outpatients

Note. BT = behavior therapy; SSRIs = selective serotonin reuptake inhibitors; Y-BOCS = Yale-Brown Obsessive Compulsive Scale.
[a] Subjects had subclinical OCD at follow-up (i.e., obsessions/compulsions present but not at full criteria). [b] Three of the six subjects in remission (i.e., symptom free) were receiving medication. [c] Course assessed by percentage change in Y-BOCS score only.

chiatric Rating Scale (PSR; Keller et al. 1987) for OCD. The PSR rates symptom severity on a 6-point scale ranging from a high of 6 (severely symptomatic and unable to function at work and socially) to a low of 0 (no OC symptoms or avoidance). Follow-up measures were obtained at 3 months, 6 months, 1 year, and 2 years after baseline assessment.

Course of illness was assessed both descriptively and with survival analysis to determine probability of remission and relapse. Of the 51 subjects who started the study meeting full criteria for OCD (Y-BOCS score greater than 16), 57% still met full criteria after 2 years. Although some of these subjects had considerable improvement in the severity of their OC symptoms, they nonetheless continued to experience significant impairment because of obsessions and/or compulsions. Twelve percent had minimal or no symptoms (Y-BOCS scores below 8). The remainder of the subjects (31%) had obsessions and compulsions that persisted but did not meet full criteria, and thus might be classified as being in partial remission or much improved.

Statistical analysis with survival analysis revealed a 47% probability of achieving at least partial remission during the 2-year study period. However, if more stringent criteria were used to define remission, in which patients must have had only occasional or no obsessions and compulsions for 8 consecutive weeks (Y-BOCS score below 8), there was only a 12% probability of achieving remission. Once in remission, the probability of subsequent relapse (returning to a Y-BOCS score greater than 16) was 48%. Of the 22 patients who achieved partial remission, 10 patients relapsed and 12 patients remained in partial remission throughout the study.

Another prospective study examined 107 clinic patients with OCD followed up to 5 years after intake (G. Steketee, J. Eisen, I. Dyck, M. Warshaw, and S. Rasmussen, "Predictors of Course of OCD" [submitted for publication]). The probability of full remission for at least a 2-month period was .22 at 5 years, with a probability of .53 for partial remission. Interestingly, the likelihood of improvement increased substantially with time, doubling from the 6-month point (.27) to the 5-year point (.53). Although outcome in this study was assessed with only a 3-point rating scale, the study findings are very similar to those reported by Eisen and colleagues (1995b), who, as previously noted, used the PSR and the Y-BOCS.

These findings are in keeping with those of most of the retrospective and prospective studies of OCD, which demonstrate that the majority of people who meet full criteria for this disorder continue to suffer from obsessions and compulsions, although they may experience considerable improvement in both the intensity of their symptoms and the corresponding degree of impairment. Those fortunate subjects who experience complete remission of their OC symptoms are very much in the minority.

Effect of Treatment on Course of Illness

A follow-up study of children with OCD was conducted by Leonard et al. (1993) to determine outcome after standardized short-term treatment with clomipramine (a medication known to be effective in OCD). Fifty-four children and adolescents were reinterviewed 2–7 years after participation in a controlled trial of clomipramine and a variety of interim interventions. At follow-up the majority of patients were only mildly symptomatic, and OC symptoms were more severe in only 10 subjects at reassessment, so that, as a whole, the cohort had improved. However, only 3 subjects (6%) were considered to be in true remission (defined as experiencing no obsessions or compulsions and receiving no medication), whereas 23 subjects (43%) still met full criteria for OCD (see Table 14–2). In addition, the majority of patients were taking medication at follow-up, which suggests that maintenance of improvement in OCD may require ongoing pharmacological intervention.

In a 1994 study conducted by Orloff et al., findings were more optimistic than those in the studies described above. Of 85 subjects assessed 1–3 years after baseline evaluation, 64% had a greater than 50% decrease in Y-BOCS score and 33% had a greater than 75% decrease in Y-BOCS score. The mean follow-up Y-BOCS score (10.1 ± 7.0) showed mild to minimal obsessions and compulsions that did not interfere with functioning. This improvement in OC symptoms may be the result of the availability of current, effective behavioral and pharmacological treatments for OCD that use exposure and response prevention techniques and selective serotonin reuptake inhibitors (SSRIs). In fact, nearly all subjects had received at least a 10-week trial of an SSRI, and almost half had received some behavior therapy (BT) (although only 16% had received at least 20 hours of BT). Of note are the findings that most patients were still taking medication at follow-up and that there were clear relapses in those patients who had discontinued their medication. Again, maintenance of improvement of OC symptoms over time appeared to require continued treatment.

The effect of treatment on course of illness in OCD was also evaluated in the previously described prospective 2-year follow-up of 68 subjects conducted by Eisen et al. (1995b). Among this group, a large percentage had received at least 12 weeks of a serotonergic medication: 49% received clomipramine, 29%, fluvoxamine, and 15%, fluoxetine, and some had received more than one SSRI. Patients took medication for 70 weeks on average. Thus, 84% of the total sample received an adequate trial of at least one SSRI during the study period. Patients were considered to have received adequate BT if their therapist had used exposure and response prevention and they had spent at least 20 hours practicing homework assignments. According to this definition, only 18% of patients had received adequate BT.

The mean GAS and Y-BOCS scores at intake and at 2 years were similar for subjects who had and who had not received adequate trials of an SSRI. However, patients who subsequently received adequate BT over the course of the study had worse initial functioning than those without BT, and they had improved more at 2 years. In effect, these patients "caught up" and functioned as well as those who did not have BT at the end of the trial.

If Orloff et al.'s (1994) method is used to assess outcome, the results of this study are not as optimistic about the course of illness in OCD. Only 9% of the subjects had more than a 75% decrease in Y-BOCS scores over the 2 years, whereas 26% reported 50%–75% improvement, 23% had 25%–49% improvement, and 35% improved less than 25%. For 7%, OC symptoms worsened. However, the results again support the findings of most previous studies that even with adequate pharmacotherapy, course of illness in OCD is usually continuous, with fluctuations in severity. Few people (only about 10%–12%) achieve true remission of symptoms.

Predictors of Course

Demographic and Clinical Features

Other retrospective studies found that improvement in OCD course was associated with shorter duration of illness (Goodwin et al. 1969; Ingram 1961; Kringlen 1965; Pollitt 1957). Findings concerning whether age at onset (or presence/absence of childhood symptoms) was predictive of subsequent course were inconsistent, as were findings regarding the predictive value of marital status or of obsessional premorbid personality. However, a recent study of a large clinical sample indicated that those who were married and who had better general functioning were more likely to show symptom improvement up to 5 years later (G. Steketee, J. Eisen, I. Dyck, M. Warshaw, and S. Rasmussen, "Predictors of Course of OCD" [submitted for publication]). Type of symptoms consistently did not appear to influence course across studies (Ingram 1961; Kringlen 1965; Pollitt 1957). Summarizing these studies, Goodwin et al. (1969) concluded that short duration of symptoms prior to treatment and good premorbid personality were both associated with better prognosis. The content of obsessions did not influence outcome.

More recent studies have identified a number of factors that may influence outcome or course of illness in OCD. In one follow-up study of childhood-onset OCD, the presence of signs of puberty in males at the time of referral indicated a better prognosis (Thomsen 1995). Several studies consistently found that severity of symptoms at baseline, family history of affective or anxiety disorders, and baseline demographic variables (gender, age at onset, duration of illness at baseline, age at initial assessment) did not predict severity of OCD at follow-up (Flament et al. 1990; Leonard et al. 1993). Inconsistent results have been reported regarding the predictive value of initial good response to clomipramine and presence of neurological symptoms: Flament et al. (1990) found no effect from these factors, whereas Leonard et al. (1993) found that severity of OC symptoms after 5 weeks of clomipramine treatment was a strong predictor both of severity of OCD and of functioning at follow-up. (Similar findings have been reported for behavioral treatment of adults [e.g., Foa et al. 1983; Steketee 1993].) Interestingly, the presence of a tic disorder predicted more severe OC symptoms at follow-up in children.

In the recent studies of factors influencing course of illness in adults with OCD, some findings are consistent with those of studies of OCD in children discussed above. Several studies found that the following variables did not affect outcome: severity of depression at baseline, age at onset, duration of follow-up, presence of a personality disorder, total number of personality disorders diagnosed, adequacy of pharmacotherapy or behavioral therapy, and presence of a current affective or anxiety disorder (Eisen et al. 1995b; Orloff et al. 1994; G. Steketee, J. Eisen, I. Dyck, M. Warshaw, and S. Rasmussen, "Predictors of Course of OCD" [submitted for publication]). Eisen et al. (1995b) found a trend for subjects whose OC symptoms were improved at 3 months (25% decrease in Y-BOCS score) to be significantly more likely to achieve remission 2 years later. In that study, probability of remission was not different for OCD patients with or without comorbid tic disorders, perhaps because of the small number of patients with OCD plus tics.

Insight is another clinical feature that has been assessed as a potential predictor of course of illness in OCD. An awareness of the senselessness or unreasonableness of obsessions (often referred to as "insight") and the accompanying struggle against the obsessions (referred to as "resistance") have been generally accepted as fundamental to the diagnosis of OCD. However, numerous descriptions of OCD patients who are completely convinced of the reasonableness of their obsessions and who need to enact compulsions have appeared in the psychiatric literature during the past century. In 1986, Insel and Akiskal described several such patients and presented the hypothesis that patients with OCD have varying degrees of insight and resistance, with "obsessive-compulsive psychosis" at one extreme of a hypothesized continuum. They also noted a fluidity between "neurotic" (i.e., associated with insight) and psychotic states in these patients.

To reflect these clinical observations and research findings, which have established that a range of insight exists in OCD (Foa and Kozak 1995; Kozak and Foa 1994; Lelliott et al. 1988), DSM-IV designated a new OCD specifier—"with poor insight," applying to individuals who generally fail to recognize their obsessions and compulsions as excessive or irrational. Eisen and Rasmussen (1993) retrospectively assessed course of illness in four categories of patients: those with OCD and schizophrenia (n = 18), OCD and schizotypal personality disorder (n = 14), OCD with poor insight (n = 27), and OCD without psychotic features (n = 408). High percentages of both the schizophrenia (82%) and the schizotypal (69%) groups had a deteriorative course. In contrast, very few of the OCD patients with poor insight (17%) and without psychotic features (8%) had a worsening course. Although these results need to be replicated with more rigorous methodology, the findings suggest that lack of insight does not significantly affect course of illness.

Axis I and II Comorbidity

The presence of other concurrent anxiety disorders has been examined in only one prospective study of course in clinic patients (G. Steketee, J. Eisen, I. Dyck, M. Warshaw, and S. Rasmussen, "Predictors of Course of OCD" [submitted for publication]). Surprisingly, having another anxiety disorder was actually protective; those with more comorbid anxiety disorders were more likely to improve. Perhaps the presence of other anxiety disorders, which may have been predominant over OCD symptoms in these patients, signaled a general vulnerability to anxiety that could change focus to other content, reducing obsessive and compulsive complaints.

Welner et al. (1976) compared the clinical pictures via chart review before, during, and after hospitalization of 150 patients with OCD. Their sample was divided into five subgroups: 1) OCD only (20%), 2) OCD followed by depression (developing an average of 14 years later) (38%), 3) concurrent onset of OCD and depression (13%), 4) primary depression with subsequent development of OCD (11%), and 5) OCD associated with other disorders. Clearly, depressive symptoms developing long after OCD onset was the predominant pattern. Patients with this history had an earlier age at OCD onset, a longer duration of illness, and less frequent and shorter remissions than patients in other groups. Patients with OCD only also had an earlier onset of OCD than did those in the concurrent depression onset group. The "primacy" of OCD over depression thus seemed associated with earlier onset and greater chronicity, a finding in agreement with the results of several other studies (see also Coryell 1981; Gittleson 1966b; Lion 1942; Stengel 1991). In contrast, the "primacy" of depression over OCD, which might include concurrent onset of both, was associated with a more episodic course, as one might predict given the seemingly different course characteristics of depression.

The co-occurrence of OCD with bipolar disorder is much less common than that with unipolar depression, no doubt in part because bipolar disorder is less common in general than unipolar depression. However, clinical reports (Keck et al. 1986; Gordon and Rasmussen 1988) have suggested that when bipolar disorder and OCD coexist, the OC symptoms may become exacerbated during depression but resolve completely during mania. This circumstance may contribute to some of the disparate results described below on the prognostic implications of OCD in the context of psychotic disorders, including alleged schizophrenia.

Several investigators have examined the prognostic implications of psychotic features in OCD. For schizophrenic individuals with OCD, both Stengel (1991) and Rosen (1957) determined that preexisting OCD symptoms predicted a more benign course for the schizophrenia. Interestingly, in the latter study, in no case did onset of schizophrenia precede onset of OCD, and in most cases OC symptoms persisted unchanged after onset of schizophrenia. However, the marked depressive symptoms present in most of the patients may have accounted for the better prognoses, given that such symptoms typically remit with time. In contradiction to these reports, Fenton and McGlashan (1986) found that the presence of OCD contributed to worse outcome in schizophrenic inpatients who were followed retrospectively 16 years after intake. Otherwise, the combined group resembled other schizophrenic patients at admission except for earlier onset of illness, an obvious contributor to chronicity. The authors were able to determine that OC symptoms came first in 13 of the 21 cases; in other cases, no determination regarding onset could be made. Thus, whether earlier onset of OC symptoms predicted a worse course is unclear. Given that diagnostic precision in this study is undoubtedly better than that in the earlier reports, these findings may be more accurate.

A few investigators have attempted to relate various personality traits to course of illness. Inconsistent results have been reported concerning the presence of compulsive personality traits: both positive and negative effects have been described. Kendell and Discipio (1970) characterized 45% of their 60 depressed inpatients as having premorbid "obsessional traits." These obsessional depressive patients did not show as much reduction in OC symptom scores after recovery from depression as did other depressed patients. On the other hand, Lo (1967) reported that premorbid obsessional personality predicted more favorable outcome of OCD at 4-year follow-up. This positive influence has also been reported in the behavioral treatment literature (Boulougouris 1977).

More consistent results have been found concerning schizotypal personality disorder. Its presence predicted a less favorable course of OCD in several studies (Orloff et al. 1994; Eisen and Rasmussen 1993) as well as a poorer treatment response.

Predictors of Behavioral and Pharmacological Treatment Outcome

Findings regarding variables that affect the long-term outcome of treatment, both behavioral and pharmacological, may have some bearing on the course of illness for this disorder.

Demographic and Clinical Features

Relatively few demographic variables have been found to influence treatment outcome. Current age did not predict the outcome of behavioral (e.g., Hoogduin and Duivenvoorden 1988; O'Sullivan et al. 1991; Rabavilas et al. 1976) or pharmacological treatment (e.g., Ackerman et al. 1994). In contrast to studies of course and findings for drug treatment trials (e.g., Ackerman et al. 1994; Ravizza et al. 1995), OCD patients with earlier symptom onset maintained their gains better after behavioral treatment than did those with later symptom onset (Emmelkamp et al. 1985; Foa et al. 1983). Gender did not affect OCD symptoms over time for behavioral or medication treatment (Ackerman et al. 1994; Boulougouris 1977; Drummond 1993; Hoogduin and Duivenvoorden 1988; O'Sullivan et al. 1991; Ravizza et al. 1995), although Basoglu et al. (1988) observed that women with washing rituals fared better than men with such rituals at follow-up. Unfortunately, gender in that study was confounded with symptom type and appeared to influence depressed mood more than OCD symptoms. Marital status was not related to pharmacological or behavioral treatment outcome (Foa et al. 1983; Hoogduin and Duivenvoorden 1988; Ravizza et al. 1995), nor were education level (Hoogduin and Duivenvoorden 1988) or whether patients lived alone or with others (Foa et al. 1983). Greater work satisfaction was related to more enduring gains (Mawson et al. 1982), but it is likely that this variable reflects better overall functioning. Not surprisingly, lower income was associated with poorer outcome (Steketee 1993; Steketee et al. 1985).

As in studies of course of OCD, symptom severity was not predictive of long-term outcome in most behavioral and drug studies (Ackerman et al. 1994; Basoglu et al. 1988; Foa et al. 1983; Hoogduin and Duivenvoorden 1988; Marks et al. 1980; O'Sullivan et al. 1991), indicating that severity alone does not necessarily signal a poor prognosis. However, it does seem likely that more severe symptoms will also be associated with more functional impairment—and perhaps with more comorbid conditions—and that this combination of factors will adversely affect treatment outcome. This hypothesis remains to be tested, although one study of response to SSRI medication showed that episodic course and no previous hospitalizations, which might be expected to signal better functioning and less severity, did indeed predict a good outcome

(Ravizza et al. 1995). However, in the only study we could locate that actually examined level of functioning in OCD, pretreatment functioning did not predict follow-up BT outcome (Steketee 1993). Surprisingly, the duration of symptoms was also not predictive in any study (Cottraux et al. 1993; Foa et al. 1983; Hoogduin and Duivenvoorden 1988; O'Sullivan et al. 1991), although again it is possible that chronicity accompanied by comorbidity may worsen prognosis. As was the case for studies of course, type of ritual (washing versus checking) was unrelated to outcome in most behavioral studies (Foa et al. 1983; Rachman et al. 1973) and medication trials (e.g., Ackerman et al. 1994). This factor had erratic predictive value in other behavioral studies (Basoglu et al. 1988; Drummond 1993), thus arguing against any consistent relationship of symptom type to outcome.

Mood State and Comorbid Conditions

Researchers have disagreed strongly over the role of depression in OCD. In some behavioral studies, patients who were more depressed before therapy had improved less at follow-up (Foa et al. 1983; Keijers et al. 1994) and were taking more medications 6 years later (Jenike 1990; O'Sullivan et al. 1991). Furthermore, better outcome was observed in depressed OCD patients who received medication (Cottraux et al. 1993; Marks et al. 1980). On the other hand, depression failed to predict outcome in many other behavioral studies (see Steketee and Shapiro 1995 for a review) as well as in pharmacological trials (e.g., Ravizza et al. 1995). Likewise, in a prospective study, Foa and colleagues (1992) found that neither baseline depression level nor implementation of effective antidepressant intervention predicted outcome at follow-up.

Interestingly, one study examined the predictive value of OCD patients' histories of mood fluctuations prior to treatment (Rabavilas and Boulougouris 1979). The absence of mood changes was associated with more improvement at follow-up, whereas the presence of mood fluctuations predicted relapse over time. In studies of the influence of diagnosed major depressive disorders on OCD outcome, no relationship was observed in outcome after BT (Steketee et al. 1995) or SSRI medication (e.g., Goodman et al. 1989; Pigott et al. 1991). Unfortunately, this body of research leaves considerable uncertainty regarding the importance of depressed mood in patients with OCD. Whether antidepressant medication should be used in such patients to manage the depression is far from clear, but such use might be advisable in severe cases.

Findings for pretreatment levels of anxious mood in OCD are somewhat consistent, although not entirely so. No significant association was observed in the majority of behavioral and medication studies of follow-up outcome (e.g., Emmelkamp et al. 1985; Orloff et al. 1994;

O'Sullivan et al. 1991; Ravizza et al. 1995; Steketee 1988). In contrast, both Foa et al. (1983) and Visser et al. (1992) found that greater initial anxiety predicted worse BT outcome. However, the path of this association was not direct in Foa's study, and the variance accounted for was quite small in the Visser et al. study. The effects of comorbid generalized anxiety disorder (GAD) on OCD outcome at 6-month follow-up were more negative. Steketee et al. (1995) noted that all four of their patients with this condition failed to benefit from BT. It seems, then, that whereas general anxious mood is unlikely to pose a problem, concurrent GAD may do so. Other anxiety comorbidity such as panic disorder has not been studied, but clinical experience suggests that concurrent treatment for panic symptoms that appear in response to obsessive focus will be needed, particularly during exposure treatment.

The presence of any personality disorder did not predict outcome for OCD patients after BT (Steketee 1991; Steketee et al. 1995) or SSRI medication (Orloff et al. 1994). However, Aubuchon and Malatesta (1994) found that OCD patients with comorbid personality disorders tended to drop out of and to be more difficult to manage during therapy. Furthermore, particular types of personality disorders, such as avoidant, borderline, and paranoid personality disorders (Cottraux et al. 1993; Jenike 1990), as well as passive-aggressive personality traits (Steketee 1991), have predicted poor outcome. Compliance was a problem for all eight of Hermesh et al.'s (1987) borderline personality disorder patients, who failed to respond to BT or clomipramine. Likewise, Rasmussen and Tsuang (1987) concurred that borderline, as well as histrionic, OCD patients responded poorly to treatment, although these authors provided no data to support their contention. Steketee et al. (1995) observed that dramatic-cluster traits were marginally correlated with 6-month outcome, but this association disappeared when other variables were considered. Jenike and colleagues (1986; Minichiello et al. 1987) reported that, in contrast to nonschizotypal patients, 90% of whom improved at least moderately with behavioral treatment or medications, only 7% of schizotypal patients showed lasting gains. Further, the number of schizotypal traits correlated strongly with negative outcome $(r = -.74)$. Ravizza et al. (1995) reported similar findings for response to clomipramine or fluoxetine. Overall, then, although a number of personality disorders appear to be benign accompaniments to OCD, others (e.g., borderline or schizotypal personality disorder) are likely to present problems for long-term OCD course.

Whether insight is an important predictor of prognosis and treatment response in OCD is an intriguing question that has received little investigation. The few available reports are conflicting. One study noted that patients with overvalued ideas did not respond as well to BT as did those with good insight (Foa 1979), but another study reported that patients with high conviction about their obsessions and the need to enact compulsions responded well to behavioral intervention (Lelliott et al. 1988). This latter finding was also reported in a study that assessed insight as a potential predictor of response to sertraline (Eisen et al. 1995a). A rating scale developed to evaluate degree of insight and conviction, the Brown Assessment of Beliefs Scale (BABS; J. L. Eisen, K. A. Philips, D. Beer, S. A. Rasmussen, and L. Baer, unpublished, 1994), was administered to 38 OCD subjects before and after a 16-week open trial of sertraline. Poor insight did not predict response to medication. It is clear that more research will be needed to determine the effect of insight and of variables associated with poor insight on course.

Summary

In keeping with the older literature, several more recent studies using a prospective design, standardized criteria to assess diagnosis, and structured interviews with direct patient contact have shown that the majority of patients either continue to meet full criteria for the disorder or retain significant OC symptoms. This finding has also been supported in several prospective studies of children with OCD. In all these studies examining changes in severity of OC symptoms over time, the effect of treatment on the course of illness has not been firmly established. However, several recent prospective studies suggest that appropriate pharmacological treatment may improve outcome only while the patient continues to receive this treatment (Leonard et al. 1993; Orloff et al. 1994).

Factors that contribute to the course of illness severity in OCD have been assessed in many retrospective as well as prospective studies. Determining which variables influence the likelihood of remission or worsening of symptoms is clinically useful and may enhance our understanding of the underlying processes involved in OCD.

According to both course and treatment literature on predictors of follow-up outcome for OCD, surprisingly few demographic and clinical features, including severity and duration of symptoms, consistently predict outcome at follow-up. Even the role of age at onset is uncertain, given that early onset has been associated with poorer response in some studies and with better response in others. Onset age may interact with gender, so that boys/men with early-onset OCD fare worse than do girls/women, perhaps because of other associated features such as personality traits. More careful research to clarify these points are needed, especially if early intervention methods are to be guided by research findings.

The role of general functioning variables in long-term gains is less certain, since some studies suggest that poor adjustment negatively influences maintenance of gains. Neither depressed nor anxious mood have been found to be definitive predictors of outcome, although the former remains a question, and studies of OCD patients with comorbid major depressive disorder are needed. There is remarkably little information about the effect of comorbid anxiety disorders on outcome. Because OCD rarely occurs in the absence of other Axis I conditions, it is important to know whether any of these consistently affect treatment outcome. The predictive utility of comorbid personality disorders is far from established, given the paucity of research in this area. However, some personality styles appear to be potentially problematic, including schizotypal personality and possibly passive-aggressive, borderline, and paranoid personality disorder. Considerably more research on these comorbid conditions and their specific effects is needed.

References

Ackerman D, Greenland S, Bystritsky A, et al: Predictors of treatment response in obsessive-compulsive disorder: multivariate analyses from a multicenter trial of clomipramine. J Clin Psychopharmacol 14:247–254, 1994

American Psychiatric Association: Diagnostic and Statistical Manual of Mental Disorders, 3rd Edition, Revised. Washington, DC, American Psychiatric Association, 1987

American Psychiatric Association: Diagnostic and Statistical Manual of Mental Disorders, 4th Edition. Washington, DC, American Psychiatric Association, 1994

Apter A, Tyano S: Obsessive compulsive disorders in adolescence. Journal of Adolescence 11:183–194, 1988

Aubuchon PG, Malatesta VJ: Obsessive compulsive patients with comorbid personality disorder: associated problems and response to a comprehensive behavior therapy. J Clin Psychiatry 55:448–453, 1994

Basoglu M, Lax T, Kasvikis Y, et al: Predictors of improvement in obsessive-compulsive disorder. Journal of Anxiety Disorders 2:299–317, 1988

Berg CL, Rapoport JL, Whitaker A, et al: Childhood obsessive compulsive disorder: a two-year prospective follow-up of a community sample. J Am Acad Child Adolesc Psychiatry 28:528–533, 1989

Berman L: The obsessive-compulsive neurosis in children. J Nerv Ment Dis 95:26–39, 1942

Boulougouris J: Variables affecting the behavior of obsessive-compulsive patients treated by flooding, in Phobic and Obsessive Compulsive Disorders. Edited by Boulougouris JC, Rabavilas AD. New York, Pergamon, 1977, pp 73–84

Coryell W: Obsessive-compulsive disorder and primary unipolar depression: comparisons of background, family history, course, and mortality. J Nerv Ment Dis 169:220–224, 1981

Cottraux J, Messy P, Marks IM, et al: Predictive factors in the treatment of obsessive-compulsive disorders with fluvoxamine and/or behavior therapy. Behavioral Psychology 21:45–50, 1993

Demal U, Gerhard L, Mayrhofer A, et al: Obsessive-compulsive disorder and depression. Psychopathology 26:145–150, 1993

Drummond LM: The treatment of severe, chronic, resistant obsessive-compulsive disorder. Br J Psychiatry 163:223–229, 1993

Eisen JL, Rasmussen SA: Obsessive-compulsive disorder with psychotic features. J Clin Psychiatry 54:373–379, 1993

Eisen JL, Rasmussen SA, Goodman W: Does insight predict response to SSRIs in OCD? Poster presented at the American Psychiatric Association Annual Meeting, Miami, FL, May 1995a

Eisen JL, Rasmussen SA, Goodman W, et al: Patterns of remission and relapse: a 2-year prospective study of OCD. Poster presented at the American Psychiatric Association Annual Meeting, Miami, FL, May 1995b

Emmelkamp PMG, Hoekstra RJ, Visser A: The behavioral treatment of obsessive-compulsive disorder: prediction of outcome at 3.5-year follow-up, in Psychiatry: The State of the Art. Edited by Pichot P, Berner R, Wolf R, et al. New York, Plenum, 1985, pp 265–270

Endicott J, Spitzer RL, Fleiss JL: The Global Assessment Scale: a procedure for measuring overall severity of psychiatric disturbance. Arch Gen Psychiatry 33:766–771, 1976

Fenton WS, McGlashan TH: The prognostic significance of obsessive-compulsive symptoms in schizophrenia. Am J Psychiatry 143:437–441, 1986

Flament MF, Whitaker A, Rapoport JL, et al: Obsessive compulsive disorder in adolescence. J Am Acad Child Adolesc Psychiatry 27:764–771, 1988

Flament MF, Koby E, Rapoport JL, et al: Childhood obsessive-compulsive disorder: a prospective follow-up study. J Child Psychol Psychiatry 31:363–380, 1990

Foa EB: Failure in treating obsessive-compulsives. Behav Res Ther 17:169–176, 1979

Foa EB, Kozak MJ: DSM-IV field trial: obsessive-compulsive disorder. Am J Psychiatry 152:90–96, 1995

Foa EB, Grayson JB, Steketee GS, et al: Success and failure in the behavioral treatment of obsessive-compulsives. J Consult Clin Psychol 51:287–297, 1983

Foa EB, Kozak MJ, Steketee GS, et al: Treatment of depressive and obsessive-compulsive symptoms in OCD by imipramine and behavior therapy. J Clin Psychiatry 31:279–292, 1992

Gittleson NL: Depressive psychosis in the obsessional neurotic. Br J Psychiatry 112:883–887, 1966

Gojer J, Khanna S, Channabasaranna S, et al: Obsessive compulsive disorder, anxiety and depression. Indian Journal of Psychological Medicine 10:25–30, 1987

Goodman WK, Lawrence HP, Rasmussen SA, et al: The Yale-Brown Obsessive Compulsive Scale, I: development, use, and reliability. Arch Gen Psychiatry 46:1006–1011, 1989

Goodwin DW, Guze SB, Robins E: Follow-up studies in obsessional neurosis. Arch Gen Psychiatry 20:182–187, 1969

Gordon A, Rasmussen S: Mood-related obsessive-compulsive symptoms in a patient with bipolar affective disorder. J Clin Psychiatry 49:27–28, 1988

Grimshaw L: The outcome of obsessional disorder: a follow-up study of 100 cases. Br J Psychiatry 111:1051–1056, 1965

Hanna GL: Demographic and clinical features of obsessive-compulsive disorder in children and adolescents. J Am Acad Child Adolesc Psychiatry 34:19–27, 1995

Hermesh H, Shahar A, Munitz H: Obsessive-compulsive disorder and borderline personality disorder. Am J Psychiatry 144:120–121, 1987

Hoogduin CAL, Duivenvoorden HJ: A decision model in the treatment of obsessive-compulsive neurosis. Br J Psychiatry 144:516–521, 1988

Ingram IM: Obsessional illness in mental hospital patients. J Ment Sci 107:382–402, 1961

Insel TR, Akiskal HS: Obsessive-compulsive disorder with psychotic features: a phenomenological analysis. Am J Psychiatry 143:1527–1533, 1986

Jenike MA: Predictors of treatment failure, in Obsessive-Compulsive Disorders: Theory and Management. Edited by Jenike MA, Baer L, Minichiello WE. Chicago, IL, Year Book Medical, 1990, pp 306–311

Jenike MA, Baer L, Minichiello WE, et al: Concomitant obsessive-compulsive disorder and schizotypal personality disorders. Am J Psychiatry 143:306–311, 1986

Karno M, Golding J, Sorenson S, et al: The epidemiology of obsessive compulsive disorder in five U.S. communities. Arch Gen Psychiatry 45:1094–1099, 1988

Keck PE, Lipinski JF, White K: An inverse relationship between mania and obsessive-compulsive disorder. J Clin Psychopharmacol 6:123–124, 1986

Keijers GP, Hoogduin AL, Schaap CPDR: Predictors of treatment outcome in the behavioral treatment of obsessive-compulsive disorder. Br J Psychiatry 165:781–786, 1994

Keller MB, Lavori PW, Friedman B, et al: The Longitudinal Interval Follow-Up Evaluation: a comprehensive method for assessing outcome in prospective longitudinal studies. Arch Gen Psychiatry 44:540–548, 1987

Kendell RE, Discipio WJ: Obsessional symptoms and obsessional personality traits in patients with depressive illnesses. Psychol Med 1:65–72, 1970

Kozak MJ, Foa EB: Obsessions, overvalued ideas, and delusions in obsessive-compulsive disorder. Behavior Res Ther 32:343–353, 1994

Kringlen E: Obsessional neurotics: a long-term follow-up. Br J Psychiatry 111:709–722, 1965

Lelliott PT, Noshirvani HF, Basoglu M, et al: Obsessive-compulsive beliefs and treatment outcome. Psychol Med 18:697–702, 1988

Leonard HL, Swedo SE, Lenane MC, et al: A two- to seven-year follow-up study of 54 obsessive compulsive children and adolescents. Arch Gen Psychiatry 50:429–439, 1993

Lewis A: Problems of obsessional illness. Proc Royal Soc Medicine 29:325–336, 1936

Lion EG: Anancastic depressions: obsessive-compulsive symptoms occurring during depressions. J Nerv Ment Dis 95:730–738, 1942

Lo WH: A follow-up study of obsessional neurotics in Hong Kong Chinese. Br J Psychiatry 113:823–832, 1967

Marks IM, Stern RS, Mawson D, et al: Clomipramine and exposure for obsessive-compulsive rituals, I. Br J Psychiatry 136:1–25, 1980

Mawson D, Marks IM, Ramm L, et al: Clomipramine and exposure for chronic obsessive-compulsive rituals: two-year follow-up and further findings. Br J Psychiatry 140:11–18, 1982

Minichiello W, Baer L, Jenike MA: Schizotypal personality disorder: a poor prognostic indicator for behavior therapy in the treatment of obsessive-compulsive disorder. Journal of Anxiety Disorders 1:273–276, 1987

Orloff LM, Battle MA, Baer L, et al: Long-term follow-up of 85 patients with obsessive-compulsive disorder. Am J Psychiatry 151:441–442, 1994

O'Sullivan G, Noshirvani H, Marks I, et al: Six-year follow-up after exposure and clomipramine therapy for obsessive compulsive disorder. J Clin Psychiatry 52:150–155, 1991

Pato MT, Eisen JL, Pato CN: Rating scales for obsessive-compulsive disorder, in Current Insights in Obsessive-Compulsive Disorder. Edited by Hollander E, Zohar J, Marazziti D, et al. West Sussex, UK, John Wiley & Sons, 1994, pp 77–92

Pigott TA, Pato MT, L'Heureux F, et al: A controlled comparison of adjuvant lithium carbonate or thyroid hormone in clomipramine-treated patients with obsessive-compulsive disorder. J Clin Psychopharmacol 11:242–248, 1991

Pollitt J: Natural history of obsessional states: a study of 150 cases. BMJ 1:194–198, 1957

Rabavilas AD, Boulougouris JC: Mood changes and flooding outcome in obsessive-compulsive patients: report of a 2-year follow-up. J Nerv Ment Dis 167:495–496, 1979

Rabavilas AD, Boulougouris JC, Stefanis C: Duration of flooding sessions in the treatment of obsessive-compulsive patients. Behav Res Ther 14:349–355, 1976

Rachman S, Marks IM, Hodgson R: The treatment of obsessive-compulsive neurotics by modelling and flooding in vivo. Behav Res Ther 14:349–355, 1973

Rasmussen SA, Eisen JL: The epidemiology and clinical features of OCD. Psychiatr Clin North Am 15:743–758, 1992

Rasmussen SA, Tsuang MT: Clinical characteristics and family history in DSM-III obsessive-compulsive disorder. Am J Psychiatry 143:317–322, 1986

Rasmussen SA, Tsuang MT: Obsessive-compulsive disorder and borderline personality disorder. Am J Psychiatry 144:121–122, 1987

Ravizza L, Barzega G, Bellino S, et al: Predictors of drug treatment response in obsessive-compulsive disorder. J Clin Psychiatry 56:368–373, 1995

Rettew DC, Swedo SE, Leonard HL, et al: Obsessions and compulsions across time in 79 children and adolescents with obsessive-compulsive disorder. J Am Acad Child Adolesc Psychiatry 31:1050–1056, 1992

Rosen I: The clinical significance of obsessions in schizophrenia. J Ment Sci 103:773–785, 1957

Rosenberg CM: Complications of obsessional neurosis. Br J Psychiatry 114:477–478, 1968

Steketee G: Intra- and interpersonal characteristics predictive of long-term outcome following behavioral treatment of obsessive-compulsive disorder, in Panic and Phobias II. Edited by Hand I, Wittchen HU. Berlin, Springer-Verlag, 1988, pp 221–232

Steketee G: Personality traits and disorders in obsessive-compulsives. Journal of Anxiety Disorders 4:351–364, 1991

Steketee G: Social support and treatment outcome of obsessive compulsive disorder at 9-month follow-up. Behavioral Psychotherapy 21:81–95, 1993

Steketee G, Shapiro L: Predicting behavioral treatment outcome for agoraphobia and obsessive compulsive disorder. Clinical Psychology Review 15:317–346, 1995

Steketee G, Kozak MJ, Foa SB: Predictors and outcome for obsessive-compulsives treated with exposure and response prevention. Paper presented at the European Association for Behavior Therapy, Munich, West Germany, September 1985

Steketee G, Chambless D, Tran G, et al: Comorbidity and outcome for behaviorally treated clients with OCD and agoraphobia. Paper presented at the World Congress of Behavioral and Cognitive Therapy, Copenhagen, Denmark, July 1995

Stengel E: A study on some clinical aspects of the relationship between obsessional neurosis and psychotic reaction types. J Ment Sci 166–187, 1991

Swedo SE, Rapoport JL, Leonard H, et al: Obsessive-compulsive disorder in children and adolescents: clinical phenomenology of 70 consecutive cases. Arch Gen Psychiatry 46:335–341, 1989

Thomsen PH: Obsessive-compulsive disorder in children and adolescents: a 6- to 22-year follow-up study of social outcome. European Child and Adolescent Psychiatry 4:112–122, 1995

Visser S, Hoekstra RJ, Emmelkamp PMG: Long-term follow-up study of obsessive-compulsive patients after exposure treatment, in Perspectives and Promises of Clinical Psychology. Edited by Ehlers A, Fiegenbaum W, Florin I, et al. New York, Plenum, 1992, pp 157–170

Welner A, Reich T, Robins E, et al: Obsessive-compulsive neurosis: record, follow-up, and family studies. Compr Psychiatry 17:527–539, 1976

World Health Organization: International Classification of Diseases, 9th Revision. Geneva, Switzerland, 1977

Chapter 15

Obsessive-Compulsive Disorder in Pregnancy and the Puerperium

Susan F. Diaz, M.D., Lynn R. Grush, M.D.,
Deborah A. Sichel, M.D., and Lee S. Cohen, M.D.

Pregnancy has traditionally been thought of as a time of mental well-being. However, recent studies have indicated that some women may not be protected from depression (Gotlib et al. 1989; O'Hara 1986) or panic disorder (Cohen et al. 1994a) during pregnancy. In contrast, the puerperium has generally been recognized as a period of increased risk for the development of psychiatric illness (Kendell et al. 1981; Paffenberg 1982). Reports describing postpartum depression (O'Hara 1986) and puerperal psychosis (Kendell et al. 1981) are predominant in the literature, and panic disorder in the postpartum period has more recently been described in the literature (Cohen et al. 1994b). Little is known, however, about the natural history of obsessive-compulsive disorder (OCD) in women during pregnancy and the puerperium.

In the general population, OCD has an estimated lifetime prevalence of roughly 2%, with men and women equally affected (Karno et al. 1988). The age at onset for women tends to be the early 20s, and the course is typically continuous, with waxing and waning symptoms (Rasmussen and Eisen 1991). Symptomatic periods will therefore coexist with reproductive events and persist throughout a woman's childbearing years. In this chapter we review the literature on OCD in pregnancy and the puerperium and discuss preliminary data from a naturalistic study that followed 19 women with OCD through their pregnancies.

Epidemiology

The existing literature on OCD in pregnancy and the puerperium includes epidemiological data on rates of patients who reported OCD onset during pregnancy, studies of postpartum illnesses including OCD, and case reports that specifically examined OCD in women during pregnancy and the puerperium.

In the 1950s and 1960s, several studies attempted to describe the natural history of obsessional illness by examining large groups of patients with this disorder. Each of these reports found a relationship between the onset of obsessional symptoms and pregnancy or childbirth in a subset of the patients studied. Pollitt (1957) evaluated 150 inpatients and outpatients (63 men and 87 women) with obsessional illness. He found that 93 patients (62%) identified an event that seemed to precipitate the onset of their illness. Three of these 93 patients (3%) identified pregnancy and 7 (7%) identified childbirth as the precipitant.

In a similar study of patients with obsessional illness, Ingram (1961) described several clinical features of 89 inpatients (55 women and 34 men). Among this sample, 61 (69%) identified an event occurring within 1 year of the onset of obsessional illness that was considered to be related to the onset. Pregnancy was the most common event identified. Fifteen of the 61 patients (25%) felt that the onset of their illness was related to pregnancy. The symptoms typically reported by these patients included fear of harming the child, as well as washing and avoidance rituals involving both the mother and the child. Lo (1967), in Hong Kong, studied 88 outpatients and inpatients (64 men and 24 women) with obsessional illness. Fifty-six patients (64%) identified an event occurring within 6 months of the onset of their obsessional illness that they considered significant in triggering the symptoms. Pregnancy or childbirth was identified by 3 of these 56 patients (5%). It is not clear from these studies by Politt, Ingram, and Lo whether the patients who reported perinatal onset of obsessional illness were exclusively female or included male patients as well.

Current investigators into the phenomenology of OCD continue to report an association between the acute onset of obsessive-compulsive symptoms and the perinatal period in a subset of patients. Rasmussen and Eisen have collected clinical information on 749 patients (410 women and 339 men) with DSM-III-R (American Psychiatric Association 1987)–defined OCD. Of the 410 women evaluated, 21 (5%) identified pregnancy and 12 (3%) identified childbirth as precipitants to their illness (S. Rasmussen and J. Eisen, personal communication, March 1996).

The wide range in incidence reported by these studies may be accounted for by several factors, including lack of uniform diagnostic criteria, varying severities of illness among the patient populations, and differing methods of data collection. Nonetheless, each descriptive series consistently identified a subgroup of patients whose illness onset coincided with pregnancy or the puerperium.

Several studies that identified groups of patients with postpartum illnesses also suggested vulnerability for the onset of obsessional illness in the puerperium. Button et al. (1972) reviewed the cases of 42 psychiatric patients in whom obsessions of infanticide were the central pathological feature. Diagnoses in these patients included schizophrenic reaction (40%), depression (26%), and obsessive-compulsive reaction (16%). This 16% stands in contrast to the 1 patient with obsessional illness that Davidson and Robertson (1985) reported in their review of 82 women with postpartum illness treated as inpatients between 1946 and 1971. This patient had obsessions of drowning the child and of stabbing the child with a kitchen knife, and she reported a prior postpartum exacerbation of a similar nature.

The literature contains case reports of new-onset OCD after abortion and childbirth as well as worsening of preexisting OCD during pregnancy. Lipper and Feigenbaum (1976) described a 19-year-old woman who developed disabling preoccupations with contamination, accompanied by ritualized hand washing, following a therapeutic abortion of a 20-week-old fetus.

Brandt and Mackenzie (1987) presented a case of a 26-year-old woman with a 3-year history of OCD who, after an uneventful first pregnancy at age 20, experienced an unprecedented worsening of her illness in her second pregnancy. Her symptoms included an obsessional fear of rat germs and compulsive cleaning that rendered her unable to eat or to care for her family. She required four successive hospitalizations during the pregnancy for worsening symptoms of OCD and the development of secondary major depression. Treatment during pregnancy included electroconvulsive therapy (ECT), alprazolam, and thioridazine, none of which effectively reduced her obsessive-compulsive symptoms. Her illness improved postpartum after several weeks of treatment with clomipramine.

Sichel et al. (1993a) described the onset of OCD during the puerperium in two women, aged 30 and 34 years, both with no past psychiatric history. Each woman's illness was characterized by recurrent, intrusive thoughts of harming the child by such means as stabbing it or throwing it down the stairs or out the window. In one patient the symptoms began within 3 days of the delivery, whereas the other patient developed symptoms at 4 weeks postpartum. Both women engaged in behaviors to avoid the infant, and both improved symptomatically after treatment with fluoxetine.

In the early 1990s, three groups of researchers began to more systematically review the relationship between OCD and childbearing. Buttolph and Holland (1990) sent a questionnaire to retrospectively probe for events that precipitated the onset or worsening of obsessive-compulsive symptoms to 180 consecutively evaluated patients with OCD. Of the 39 female respondents, a striking 69% ($n = 27$) related onset or worsening of OCD to pregnancy or childbirth. Within this group of 27 women, 6 (22%) reported a new onset of obsessive-compulsive symptoms during pregnancy, and 3 (11%) reported worsening of preexisting OCD during pregnancy. Eight (30%) of the 27 women reported an onset of OCD in the puerperium as they attempted to care for the child, and 6 (22%) reported worsening of preexisting OCD in the puerperium. Ten of the 14 women with postpartum exacerbations of OCD experienced symptoms after the birth of their first child, whereas 4 had puerperal exacerbations after the birth of subsequent children. Also included in this group of 27 women were 2 who reported that their OCD worsened after miscarriages and 2 who felt that the trigger for their OCD was an inability to conceive.

Neziroglu et al. (1992) conducted a similar retrospective study in a large sample of 106 women to test their hypothesis that pregnancy is a life event that may hasten the onset of OCD. These women with OCD responded to a questionnaire assessing parity and life events associated with the onset of their illness. Fifty-nine of the 106 respondents had children. Twenty-three of these 59 (39%)—still quite a large percentage but not the 69% reported by Buttolph and Holland (1990)—reported an onset of their illness during pregnancy. Of these 23 women, 12 reported onset during their first pregnancy and 11 during subsequent pregnancies. Five childless women in the sample had had first-trimester therapeutic abortions or miscarriages. Four of these 5 reported an onset or exacerbation of OCD while pregnant. This study also found that the women without children tended to first develop OCD during adolescence, whereas the women with children developed the illness later in their 20s, around the times of their pregnancies. This finding raises the possibility that patients with OCD exacerbations related to pregnancy may represent a subgroup of patients with distinct physiological contributions—possibly neurohormonal—to their illness.

Sichel et al. (1993b) retrospectively evaluated 15 women with puerperal onset of OCD. The mean age of this sample was 32 ± 6.2 years. The women presented for treatment an average of 2.2 ± 1.2 weeks after delivery, all reporting a rapid escalation of ego-alien obsessional thoughts of harming the newborn, accompanied by generalized anxiety and disruption of the mother-infant relationship. Eight of the 15 had no prior psychiatric history, whereas 5 had previous histories of panic disorder and 2 of generalized anxiety disorder. Each patient described intrusive thoughts about harming her infant as the original source of distress, but 9 women later developed depressive symptoms 2–3 weeks after the onset of their obsessional thoughts. On presentation, their Clinical Global Impression (CGI; Guy 1976) scores[1] ranged from 5 to 7, and 10 women were hospitalized for treatment. At 1-year follow-up, 12 patients remained on antiobsessional agents and reported mild symptoms (CGI scores ranging from 1 to 3). One patient discontinued treatment without recurrence of symptoms; 2 others attempted to taper their medication but became ill again. Interestingly, the symptoms of OCD in the entire sample, both at presentation and

---

[1]The CGI scale is a 7-point scale that rates severity of disease, with 1 = not at all ill and 7 = extremely ill patients.

at follow-up, were limited to intrusive obsessional thoughts without compulsions. This finding raises the possibility that puerperal OCD may be distinct from OCD affecting nongravid women.

Review of the literature reveals the absence of prospective studies following the course of OCD during pregnancy and the puerperium. A pilot study has been performed by Sichel, Cohen, and Grush of the Perinatal and Reproductive Psychiatry Clinical Research Program at Massachusetts General Hospital (D. A. Sichel, personal communication, May 1996). In this study, 19 women with a pregravid history of OCD were followed prospectively from the first trimester to 9 months postpartum. Data from the first trimester are available for 17 subjects. Fifty-nine percent (10/17) of these women met DSM-III-R criteria for OCD. By the third trimester, 74% (14/19) of the women met OCD criteria, and by 3 months postpartum, 84% (16/19) met OCD criteria.

Consistent with Rasmussen and Eisen's (1991) data on a 70% lifetime prevalence of comorbid major depression in patients with OCD, 18 of the 19 women in this sample had a lifetime history of comorbid depression. Development of major depression during the study period occurred most commonly in the first trimester ($n = 7$) and was associated with antidepressant discontinuation in the majority of these women.

Although the sample size is small, and some of the data from early pregnancy are not available, this pilot study, like much of the retrospective data, suggests that pregnancy does not confer a protective effect for women with a prior history of OCD. In addition, the third trimester and the puerperium may be times of heightened risk for the worsening of OCD.

Etiology and Pathophysiology

Compilation of the available data suggests that, in a subpopulation of vulnerable women, OCD may begin or worsen during pregnancy or in the puerperium. Women with pregravid OCD appear to be at risk for worsening during pregnancy, particularly in the third trimester or during the postpartum period. It is still not clear what factors might predict onset or worsening. Sichel et al. (1993b) and Buttolph and Holland (1990) both point out that, given the relatively high prevalence of OCD in the general population and the mean onset of illness in the childbearing years, it cannot yet be concluded that pregnancy and childbirth are causative in the development of OCD. It has been suggested that rates of affective disorder in postpartum women may not significantly differ from rates of affective disorder in nonpuerperal women (O'Hara et al. 1990); similarly, rates of puerperal OCD may reflect the prevalence of the disorder in the general population.

However, if an association between OCD and the complex events of pregnancy and childbirth exists in a subgroup of patients, it is interesting to speculate on the etiology of this association. A wide range of possible reasons for this association have been offered in the literature, including psychodynamic factors (Button et al. 1972), behavioral explanations (e.g., inability to engage in usual avoidance strategies while caring for the child) (Brandt and Mackenzie 1987; Buttolph and Holland 1990), environmental triggers (e.g., overwhelming psychosocial stress of childbirth triggering illness) (Lo 1967), and biological etiologies (Sichel et al. 1993b; Stein et al. 1993).

Understanding how biological factors affect psychiatric disorders is the focus of much research today. Several investigators have suggested that OCD may be neurohormonally modulated. There is strong evidence to suggest that the serotonin system plays a central role in OCD (Murphy et al. 1989) and some evidence that changes in estrogen can alter serotonergic binding sites (Biegor et al. 1983; Ehrenkranz 1976) and that serotonergic neurotransmission may be partially modulated by changes in estrogen and progesterone (Stockert and deRobertis 1985). The fluctuations in estrogen and progesterone during pregnancy and the puerperium may influence serotonergic function, resulting in the onset or exacerbation of obsessive-compulsive symptoms.

Oxytocin has also been hypothesized to play a role in the production of obsessive-compulsive symptoms (Altemus et al. 1994; Leckman et al. 1994; Swedo et al. 1992). Among children with OCD, Swedo et al. (1992) reported a positive correlation between cerebrospinal fluid (CSF) oxytocin levels and depressive symptoms, and in the same subjects, Altemus et al. (1994) found that treatment with clomipramine increased CSF levels of oxytocin. Leckman and colleagues (1994) found a marked elevation in CSF oxytocin levels in a subgroup of OCD patients who were medication-free, and correlated the severity of their obsessive-compulsive symptoms to the CSF oxytocin levels. Oxytocin is essential in late pregnancy and the postpartum period, as it promotes uterine contractions and lactation. One might speculate that increased concentrations of oxytocin late in pregnancy and in the postpartum period may be influential in the onset of perinatal OCD.

Prolactin is another neuropeptide whose levels rise throughout the course of pregnancy and remain elevated during lactation. Prolactin levels have been hypothesized to reflect pre- and postsynaptic serotonergic activity by Hanna et al. (1991). Their study of 18 children and adolescents with severe OCD found that prolactin levels prior to treatment with medication were negatively correlated with the duration and severity of obsessive-compulsive symptoms, whereas treatment with clomipramine significantly increased prolactin levels. The role of androgens in producing obsessive-compulsive symptoms has been questioned by Casas et al. (1986). They treated four OCD patients with cyproterone acetate, a potent antiandrogen, and noted a remission in symptoms.

In addition to research relating hormonal changes to obsessive-compulsive symptoms, several clinical observations have also pointed to hormonal fluctuations as one factor in the onset of obsessive-compulsive symptoms. Puberty is the time when girls who develop OCD typically experience symptoms for the first time. In children under the age of 10, boys with OCD outnumber girls 7 to 1; after puberty, the sex ratio shifts to 1 : 1.5 (Swedo et al. 1989). Among adults with OCD, Rasmussen and Eisen (1991) observed that 60% of the 138 women in their clinically derived sample reported worsening of their obsessive-compulsive symptoms premenstrually.

Research into the effects of hormones on OCD is quite preliminary at this time. However, these early observations raise the possibility that neurohormonal fluctuations, including those that occur during pregnancy and the puerperium, may affect neurotransmitter activity and result in the behavioral and psychic symptoms of OCD.

Treatment Recommendations

Women with OCD should be closely monitored throughout pregnancy and into the puerperium for exacerbations of obsessive-compulsive symptoms as well as symptoms of comorbid major depression. In addition, the clinician should be aware of the potential for onset of OCD in a previously healthy woman during pregnancy or the postpartum period. In this section we first present recommendations for the clinical management of women with OCD who wish to conceive or who present during pregnancy, and then provide some clinical examples of the use of these treatments.

Preconception Counseling

Women in their reproductive years who have a history of OCD should be informed that their disorder may worsen during pregnancy and the postpartum period. They should be encouraged to use adequate contraceptive methods until they are ready to conceive. Once ready to conceive, potential treatment options and psychosocial stressors and supports should be reviewed. Treatment plans may need to be modified to increase or add cognitive-behavioral therapy (CBT) and/or supportive psychotherapy. The risk of medication use during pregnancy, as well as the risk of its discontinuation, should be discussed.

Pregnancy

First-trimester worsening of OCD symptoms or comorbid depressive symptoms may occur, particularly if pharmacotherapy is discontinued just before conception or early in the pregnancy. This worsening may be a withdrawal effect from the medication or may reflect monoamine dysregulation secondary to the acute endocrinological changes of the first trimester. Unless symptoms are severe and incapacitating, other therapies should be maximized before pharmacotherapy is introduced in the first trimester. Our experience and preliminary data suggest that obsessive-compulsive symptoms and comorbid depressive symptoms often improve in the second trimester. Conversely, our experience and preliminary data suggest that the third trimester is a period of increased vulnerability for worsening of obsessive-compulsive symptoms, although perhaps not comorbid depressive symptoms. Patients may require pharmacotherapy at this time, in addition to psychotherapy.

Postpartum

Women with pregravid OCD or circumscribed postpartum OCD may demonstrate worsening of the disorder within the first 6 weeks postpartum. If pharmacotherapy has been deferred during pregnancy, reintroduction at this time is usually necessary to treat both worsening OCD and comorbid mood disorders. The selective serotonin reuptake inhibitor antidepressants and clomipramine are the mainstays of treatment. Doses have typically been higher than those used to treat postpartum affective disorders (see Chapter 12, "Obsessive-Compulsive Disorder in Adults," in this section).

Specific Treatments

Psychotherapy

Psychodynamic and supportive therapies have not been found to be efficacious in the treatment of OCD. However, given the psychosocial stress of pregnancy and the importance of psychosocial supports during this time, these therapies remain an important intervention, although not specifically to target obsessive-compulsive symptoms.

CBT is an effective treatment for OCD and may be the only treatment required for pregnant women with mild obsessive-compulsive symptoms. It should always be considered as part of the treatment for more severe cases of OCD in pregnancy. In the general population, CBT has been shown to be effective as an adjunct to treatment with pharmacotherapy and may permit lower doses of OCD-specific pharmacotherapy (Baer and Minichiello 1990). However, studies of CBT's efficacy during pregnancy have not been reported.

Pharmacotherapy

Identification of drugs that are effective against OCD has greatly improved the lives of many OCD sufferers. The mainstays of treatment are the serotonin reuptake inhibitors clomipramine and fluoxetine, with fluvoxamine a recent addition. The question of whether or not to continue medication during pregnancy remains a dilemma, one whose risks and benefits must be carefully weighed. The extent to which medication discontinuation may worsen maternal symptoms of OCD, potentially endangering the mother and fetus, must be weighed against the potential teratological effects of prenatal antidepressant exposure.

Altshuler et al. (1996) recently reviewed the literature on the use of psychotropic medication in pregnancy. In reviewing the data on first-trimester exposure to tricyclic antidepressants (TCAs), they report that there is not a significant association between fetal exposure to TCAs and high rates of congenital malformations. They note, however, that the data are largely retrospective and are available only on a relatively small number of subjects (*n* = 414). Except for clomipramine, the TCAs do not generally provide efficacy in the treatment of OCD. Similarly, retrospective reviews indicate that exposure to fluoxetine in the first trimester does not appear to increase the risk of congenital malformations (Goldstein 1995; Pastuszak et al. 1993; Shader 1992). No data exist regarding prenatal fluvoxamine exposure.

Data regarding neonatal toxicity after in utero exposure to antidepressant medication are sparse, relying mostly on case reports and retrospective reviews. Transient withdrawal syndromes have been described in infants exposed to imipramine and nortriptyline (Eggermont 1973; Shearer et al. 1972; Webster 1973). Prenatal clomipramine exposure has resulted in cases of infant hypothermia, respiratory acidosis, and seizures (Ben Musa and Smith 1979; Cowe et al. 1982; Schimmell et al. 1991; Zahle Ostergaard and Pedersen 1982).

There are minimal prospective data on the use of psychotropics in pregnancy. Misri and Sivertz (1991) prospectively studied women with pregravid major depression who were treated with TCAs during their pregnancies. Nine women conceived while taking a TCA. Of the nine infants born to these women, none displayed any physical malformations, but one exhibited transient hypotonia and mild irritability. Nine mothers took tricyclics from the second or third trimester until delivery. Eight of the nine infants born to these women displayed withdrawal symptoms, including irritability, transient cyanosis, hypotonia, poor sucking, and tachypnea. This study is limited by its small sample size, lack of suitable control subjects, and nonstandardized assessments of infant development.

Goldstein (1995) prospectively studied the outcomes of pregnancies reported to Eli Lilly in which exposure to fluoxetine had occurred in the third trimester. One hundred and fifteen infants were identified prenatally, 89 of which had been exposed to fluoxetine during all three trimesters. Among this latter group, the rate of congenital malformations was 3.5%, which is consistent with the rate seen in the general population. Among the entire sample, transient neonatal complications were reported in 15 infants and included irritability, hyperbilirubinemia, and somnolence. Limitations of this study included the facts that the outcome data were obtained from the initial reporter of the exposure, and that there were no suitable control subjects or standardized assessments of infant development.

Remarkably few data exist regarding long-term neurobehavioral effects in children after in utero exposure to antidepressants. One small group of children exposed to TCAs in utero demonstrated normal motor skills and behavioral development at age 3 (Misri and Sivertz 1991).

For the patient requiring pharmacological treatment for OCD during pregnancy, fluoxetine appears to be the safest choice. It must be made clear to the patient that although the rate of congenital malformations may not be increased with fluoxetine use in pregnancy, the neurobehavioral effects of prenatal exposure on the neonate and in the child over the long term have not been well studied. Given the case reports of clomipramine withdrawal syndromes, it seems prudent to avoid clomipramine exposure during pregnancy. If clomipramine is used in pregnancy, consideration should be given to a slow taper prior to delivery, and the pediatrician should be notified of the possibility of clomipramine withdrawal in the infant.

Clonazepam may be considered for treating pregnant women with OCD whose anxiety is disabling. In their review of the data on first-trimester exposure to benzodiazepines, Altshuler et al. (1996) note a small absolute risk (<1%) of oral clefts. One prospective study found no maternal or neonatal compromise in 39 subjects exposed to clonazepam during pregnancy (Weinstock et al. 1996). Our clinical experience with low doses of clonazepam in pregnancy (0.5–1.5 mg) supports this study finding; however, we have observed that higher doses of clonazepam (2.0–5.0 mg) have sometimes led to adverse neonatal outcomes, such as hypotonia, apnea, and failure to feed.

The treatment of OCD during pregnancy ultimately rests on a good understanding between the patient and her physician. Patients need to be informed of the potential risks to the fetus and to themselves. The ultimate decision is the patient's, guided by the information she has received.

Clinical Examples

Patients with OCD are often secretive about their symptoms, particularly during the perinatal period, when shame and fear about being perceived as an inadequate mother may accompany the distress of the illness. The following clinical examples are designed to familiarize the clinician with ways in which the illness may present during pregnancy and the puerperium. The cases also illustrate the variability in illness course and severity during pregnancy and the postpartum period.

OCD may present for the first time during pregnancy in women who have no past psychiatric histories.

Ms. A. was a 32-year-old married woman with no prior psychiatric history. During the second trimester of her first pregnancy, she became obsessed with germs, paint, and disinfectants in her kitchen and started repeatedly washing her kitchen appliances. She would avoid going into the kitchen and using kitchen linen. Her anxiety and agitation worsened until, by 28 weeks' gestation, she avoided the kitchen altogether. Her obstetrician had reassured her that her symptoms were not of concern, and that every-thing would revert back to normal when she delivered. Eventually, Ms. A. presented for psychiatric treatment at 32 weeks' gestation in a highly agitated state. She had gained only 2 pounds during the pregnancy. She was not eating or sleeping well and was somewhat estranged from her husband, who could not understand her behavior. One week later, she went into premature labor and delivered a baby who required 3 weeks of treatment in the intensive care unit.

By the tenth postpartum week, Ms. A. had responded to a regimen of fluoxetine 40 mg and nortriptyline 75 mg. She remained on these medi-cations for a year before discontinuing them. She remained well and con-ceived again 2 years later. During the first trimester of this pregnancy, Ms. A. became mildly anxious and was treated with clonazepam 0.5 mg daily. She continued the clonazepam and supportive psychotherapy through-out the pregnancy. At 37 weeks' gestation, she delivered a healthy baby and resumed fluoxetine 20 mg daily. She remained well postpartum, with no further symptoms of OCD.

In this case, the patient experienced a new onset of OCD during her first pregnancy, with symptoms increasing to the point of incapacita-tion. One can speculate that the premature labor might have been pre-cipitated by Ms. A.'s general state of agitation and poor weight gain. Failure to recognize her illness might have contributed to the infant's prematurity and its attendant complications. Ms. A.'s second preg-nancy was notably different. She was aware of the possibility that her OCD might worsen, was treated for her anxiety, and received support-ive therapy throughout the pregnancy. The outcome for mother and baby was significantly improved.

Women may be well during one or more pregnancies yet develop OCD de novo in a subsequent pregnancy.

Ms. B. was a 30-year-old mother of a 2-year-old child. Premorbid psychi-atric symptoms were limited to obsessional traits around making lists and tidiness, but these traits had never interfered with her functioning. Ms. B. conceived quadruplets after treatment for infertility. She was advised to have a selective reduction to improve the likelihood of a healthy fetal outcome. Although this option was contrary to her beliefs, she chose to have the reduction and continued the pregnancy to term with twins.

Soon after the reduction, she became increasingly obsessive about germs. She spent excessive amounts of time cleaning and would use only one room to avoid dirtying the rest of the house. Her obsessions and compulsions made it increasingly difficult to care for her son. She subsequently became severely depressed and suicidal. Although reluctant to expose the twins to medication in utero, she elected to start fluoxetine 10 mg daily in the third trimester, which improved her symptoms only slightly.

Postpartum, while receiving fluoxetine 40 mg daily, her depression improved, but she continued to have severe obsessive-compulsive symptoms. The fluoxetine was increased to 60 mg, but Ms. B. became hypomanic. The fluoxetine was stopped while lithium was started to target the hypomania. Once her mood was stabilized, the fluoxetine was restarted. On this regimen, Ms. B.'s obsessive-compulsive symptoms improved; however, they continue to impair her functioning.

The onset of OCD during Ms. B.'s second pregnancy coincided with the stress of a voluntary reduction, which was a traumatic event for this mother. Her OCD was complicated by affective instability, necessitating the introduction of medication during pregnancy and a mood stabilizer postpartum.

Women with pregravid OCD may experience worsening of their disorder during pregnancy.

Ms. C. was a 29-year-old mother of one with a history of OCD that was treated with clomipramine 75 mg daily. On discovering her pregnancy, Ms. C. discontinued her clomipramine during the first trimester. She soon noticed an increase in her OCD symptoms, including concerns about cleanliness and compulsive hand washing and checking. By the third trimester these symptoms had worsened, and she was unable to function at home or at work. She elected to restart clomipramine during the third trimester, with a plan to taper the medication before delivery to avoid a withdrawal syndrome in the newborn. On her previous dose, Ms. C.'s symptoms improved.

Women may develop a new onset of OCD in the postpartum period after an uneventful pregnancy.

Ms. D. was a 28-year-old woman with no previous psychiatric history who had an uneventful second pregnancy. At 3 weeks postpartum, she began to experience ego-dystonic, intrusive thoughts about harming her baby. These thoughts included sexually molesting the child, throwing him down the stairs, and stabbing him with a kitchen knife. She had no compulsive behaviors. She increasingly avoided the child and lay on the couch all day. She subsequently became severely depressed and suicidal, and was hospitalized for 2 weeks.

Ms. D. was treated with fluoxetine 60 mg daily, and by 4 months postpartum the obsessive thoughts and depression were much improved. Two years later, she was free of obsessive thoughts and was gradually tapered off the fluoxetine with no symptom recurrence. She remains well but has had no further pregnancies.

In multiparas, OCD exacerbations may occur following each pregnancy, with quiescence of the illness in between pregnancies.

Ms. E. had no past psychiatric history, but presented early during the puerperium of her first pregnancy with an acute onset of intrusive, egodystonic thoughts of stabbing her infant. She was treated successfully with fluoxetine 60 mg, then tapered off medication after 1 year with no recurrence. Ms. E. subsequently had two pregnancies, during which she remained well. She developed similar intrusive thoughts after each delivery. Each postpartum episode was effectively treated with the same dose of fluoxetine. She has successfully tapered the medication without recurrence of obsessive thoughts or compulsive behaviors.

Conclusions

At present there is still much to be learned about the course of OCD in women during pregnancy and the puerperium. Controlled, prospective research is needed to clarify the rates of OCD in pregnancy and the puerperium, and to identify factors that make women more or less vulnerable to perinatal exacerbation of OCD. The extent to which a worsening of OCD in pregnancy or the postpartum period predicts a recurrence of the disorder in future pregnancies, implying a need for preventive measures in pregnancy or postpartum prophylaxis, also requires further study. Nonetheless, the clinician should be alerted to the possible emergence or exacerbation of OCD in women during pregnancy or the postpartum period.

Greater understanding is needed regarding the treatment of OCD during pregnancy and the puerperium, including the safety and efficacy of psychopharmacological treatments during pregnancy and breast feeding. Alternative modes of therapy for OCD (e.g., behavioral therapy) have not yet been studied in pregnancy and the puerperium but would likely be both efficacious and safe.

The effect of worsening obsessive-compulsive symptoms on early mother-infant relations is another unexplored area of study. Some research has shown that children of depressed mothers may develop maladaptive behaviors and experience emotional and cognitive deficits (Cogill et al. 1986; Zuckerman et al. 1990). It is possible that infants of mothers with anxiety disorders may also be vulnerable to these disturbances. If studies confirm such an association, the need for identification and intensive treatment of mothers with new or worsening OCD in the perinatal period is further underscored.

Finally, understanding the neurohormonal features that may trigger OCD in pregnancy and the puerperium could add to our understanding of the neurobiology of OCD. In addition, studies that examine the course of OCD during other times of hormonal change, such as puberty, the menstrual cycle, and menopause, would expand our knowledge and further address general issues of etiology. Taken together, this research may provide a fascinating medical model for the illness, possibly pointing toward new treatment options.

References

Altemus M, Swedo SE, Leonard HL, et al: Changes in CSF neurochemistry during treatment of OCD with clomipramine. Arch Gen Psychiatry 51:794–803, 1994

Altshuler LL, Cohen L, Szuba MP, et al: Pharmacological management of psychiatric illness during pregnancy: dilemmas and guidelines. Am J Psychiatry 153:592–606, 1996

American Psychiatric Association: Diagnostic and Statistical Manual of Mental Disorders, 3rd Edition, Revised. Washington, DC, American Psychiatric Association, 1987

Baer L, Minichiello WE: Behavioral therapy for obsessive compulsive disorder, in The Handbook of Anxiety, Vol 4. Edited by Burrows GD, Noyes R, Roth M. Amsterdam, Elsevier, 1990, pp 363–387

Ben Musa A, Smith CS: Neonatal effects of maternal clomipramine therapy (case report). Arch Dis Child 54:405, 1979

Biegor A, Reches A, Snyder L: Serotonergic and noradrenergic hormones. Life Sci 32:2015–2021, 1983

Brandt KR, Mackenzie TB: Obsessive compulsive disorder exacerbated during pregnancy: a case report. Int J Psychiatry Med 17:361–365, 1987

Buttolph ML, Holland AD: Obsessive compulsive disorders in pregnancy and childbirth, in Obsessive-Compulsive Disorders: Theory and Management. Edited by Jenike MA, Baer L, Minichiello WE. Chicago, IL, Year Book Medical, 1990, pp 89–97

Button JH, Reivich RS, Lawrence K: Obsessions of infanticide: a review of 42 cases. Arch Gen Psychiatry 27:235–240, 1972

Casas M, Alvarez E, Duro P, et al: Antiandrogenic treatment of obsessive-compulsive neurosis. Acta Psychiatr Scand 73:221–222, 1986

Cogill SR, Caplan HL, Alexandra H, et al: Impact of maternal depression on cognitive development of young children. BMJ 292:1165–1167, 1986

Cohen LS, Sichel DA, Dimmock JA, et al: Impact of pregnancy on panic disorder: a case series. J Clin Psychiatry 55:284–288, 1994a

Cohen LS, Sichel DA, Dimmock JA, et al: Postpartum course in women with preexisting panic disorder. J Clin Psychiatry 55:289–292, 1994b

Cowe L, Lloyd DJ, Dawling S: Neonatal convulsions caused by withdrawal from maternal clomipramine. BMJ 284:1837–1838, 1982

Davidson J, Robertson E: A follow-up study of postpartum illness, 1946–1978. Acta Psychiatr Scand 71:451–457, 1985

Eggermont E: Withdrawal symptoms associated with maternal imipramine therapy (case report). Lancet 2:680, 1973

Ehrenkranz JRL: Effects of sex steroids on serotonin uptake in blood platelets. Acta Endocrinol (Copenh) 83:420–428, 1976

Goldstein DJ: Effects of third trimester fluoxetine exposure on the newborn. J Clin Psychopharmacol 15:417–420, 1995

Gotlib IH, Whiffen VE, Mount JH, et al: Prevalence rates and demographic characteristics associated with depression in pregnancy and the postpartum. J Consult Clin Psychol 57:269–274, 1989

Guy W: ECDEU Assessment Manual for Psychopharmacology (DHEAW Publ No 76-338). Rockville, MD, National Institute of Mental Health, 1976

Hanna GL, McCracken JT, Cantwell DP: Prolactin in childhood OCD: clinical correlates and response to clomipramine. J Am Acad Child Adolesc Psychiatry 30:173–178, 1991

Ingram IM: Obsessional illness in mental hospital patients. J Ment Sci 107:382–402, 1961

Karno M, Goldin JM, Sorenson SB, et al: The epidemiology of OCD in five U.S. communities. Arch Gen Psychiatry 45:1094–1099, 1988

Kendell RE, McGuire RJ, Connor Y: Mood changes in the first 3 weeks after childbirth. J Affect Disord 3:317–326, 1981

Leckman JF, Goodman WK, North WG, et al: Elevated CSF levels of oxytocin in OCD. Arch Gen Psychiatry 51:782–792, 1994

Lipper S, Feigenbaum WM: Obsessive compulsive neurosis after viewing the fetus during therapeutic abortion. Am J Psychother 30:666–674, 1976

Lo WH: A follow-up study of obsessional neurotics in Hong Kong Chinese. Br J Psychiatry 113:823–832, 1967

Misri S, Sivertz K: Tricyclic drugs in pregnancy and lactation: a preliminary report. Int J Psychiatry Med 21:157–171, 1991

Murphy DL, Zohar J, Benkelfat MT, et al: OCD as a 5-HT subsystem–related behavioral disorder. Br J Psychiatry 155:15–24, 1989

Neziroglu F, Anemone R, Yaryara-Tobias JA: Onset of OCD in pregnancy. Am J Psychiatry 149:947–950, 1992

O'Hara MW: Social supports, life events and depression during pregnancy and the puerperium. Arch Gen Psychiatry 43:569–573, 1986

O'Hara MW, Zekoski EM, Philipps LK, et al: Controlled prospective study of postpartum mood disorders: comparison of childbearing and nonchildbearing women. J Abnorm Psychol 99:3–15, 1990

Paffenberg RA: Epidemiological aspects of mental illness associated with childbearing, in Motherhood and Mental Illness. Edited by Brockington IF, Kumar R. New York, Grune & Stratton, 1982, pp 19–36

Pastuszak A, Schick-Boschetto B, Zuber C, et al: Pregnancy outcome following first trimester exposure to fluoxetine (Prozac). JAMA 269:2246–2248, 1993

Pollitt J: Natural history of obsessional states: a study of 150 cases. BMJ 1:194–198, 1957

Rasmussen SA, Eisen JL: Phenomenology of OCD: clinical subtypes, heterogenicity and coexistence, in The Psychobiology of OCD. Edited by Zohar J, Insel T, Rasmussen S. New York, Springer, 1991, pp 13–43

Schimmell MS, Katz EZ, Shaag Y, et al: Toxic neonatal effects following maternal clomipramine therapy. Clin Toxicology 29:479–484, 1991

Shader RI: Does continuous use of fluoxetine during the first trimester of pregnancy present a high risk for malformation or abnormal development to the exposed fetus? J Clin Psychopharmacol 12:441, 1992

Shearer WT, Schreiner RL, Marshall RE: Urinary retention in a neonate secondary to maternal ingestion of nortriptyline. J Pediatr 81:570–572, 1972

Sichel DA, Cohen LS, Rosenbaum JF, et al: Postpartum onset of OCD. Psychosomatics 34:277–279, 1993a

Sichel DA, Cohen LS, Dimmock JA, et al: Postpartum OCD: a case series. J Clin Psychiatry 54:156–159, 1993b

Stein DJ, Hollander E, Simeon D, et al: Pregnancy and OCD. Am J Psychiatry 150:1131–1132, 1993

Stockert M, deRobertis E: Effect of ovariectomy and estrogen on [^{3}H]imipramine binding on different regions of the rat brain. Eur J Pharmacol 119:255–257, 1985

Swedo SE, Rapoport JL, Leonard H, et al: OCD in children and adolescents: clinical phenomenology of 70 consecutive cases. Arch Gen Psychiatry 46:335–341, 1989

Swedo SE, Leonard HL, Kruesi MJP, et al: CSF neurochemistry in children and adolescents with OCD. Arch Gen Psychiatry 49:29–36, 1992

Webster PAC: Withdrawal symptoms in neonates associated with maternal antidepressant therapy. Lancet 2:318–319, 1973

Weinstock LS, Cohen LS, Sichel DA, et al: Clonazepam use during pregnancy. Paper presented at the 149th Annual Meeting of the American Psychiatric Association, New York, NY, May 4–9, 1996

Zahle Ostergaard G, Pedersen SE: Neonatal effects of maternal clomipramine treatment. Pediatrics 69:233–234, 1982

Zuckerman B, Baucher H, Parker S, et al: Maternal depressive symptoms during pregnancy and newborn irritability. J Dev Behav Pediatr 11:190–194, 1990

Afterword to Section III

Michele T. Pato, M.D., and Gail Steketee, Ph.D.,
Section Editors

The diagnosis and treatment of obsessive-compulsive disorder (OCD) have come a long way in the past 20 years. OCD has gone from being a rare, untreatable illness to one that is understood to affect up to 2% of the population and that can be treated effectively—although not "cured"—from childhood through later life. However, there remain many gaps in our knowledge of the disorder, which, if filled, could play a critical role in improving treatment outcome and in identifying new methods for managing treatment-resistant and comorbid disorders. The most notable of these gaps is in our understanding of the etiology and pathophysiology of the disorder. However, new imaging techniques, genetic methods, and pharmacological probes not only promise an exciting future for investigating the causes of OCD, but also provide hope for treating individuals who are at risk for or who suffer from this debilitating illness.